STEWARDS OF LIFE

STEWARDS OF LIFE

Bioethics and Pastoral Care

Sondra Ely Wheeler

Abingdon Press
Nashville

Library of Congress Cataloging-in-Publication Data

Wheeler, Sondra Ely, 1956—
    Stewards of life : bioethics and pastoral care / Sondra Ely Wheeler.
      p.   cm.
    Includes bibliographical references.
    ISBN 0-687-02087-5 (alk. paper).
    1. Pastoral medicine.   2. Bioethics.   3. Christian ethics.
I. Title.
BV4335.W47   1996
241'.642—dc20   96-17677
                                                               CIP

This book is printed on acid-free, recycled paper.

96 97 98 99 00 01 02 03 04 05 — 10 9 8 7 6 5 4 3 2 1

MANUFACTURED IN THE UNITED STATES OF AMERICA

To

Margaret A. Farley,

my teacher in these as in many other things,

with gratitude

Contents

Preface

This book is addressed to a need within the church, one felt by congregants in general, but perhaps most acutely by ministers who serve either as pastors in local churches or as chaplains in health care settings. It is the need to respond to the moral questions generated for us by the technical capacities of modern medicine. In particular, ministers are confronted by parishioners or patients who want help in thinking through such questions, especially in understanding how their Christian faith informs or shapes judgments of this kind. As the need to make decisions about medical treatment for our parents, our spouses, and ourselves becomes more commonplace, ministers can expect to encounter requests for this sort of help more and more often. Unfortunately, many of them are ill-prepared to engage such issues, both in that they have little or no background in the language or practice of medical ethics, and in that they have not had much occasion to think in a disciplined way about the implications of Christian convictions for the care of the sick.

This volume represents an effort to introduce the language, the questions, and the methods of bioethics to those who have no prior formal acquaintance with them. It also undertakes to show why these questions should matter to Christians as such, and what distinctive contributions Christian belief can or should make to moral reflection about medical practice. Finally, it discusses the various roles a minister may be able to play in helping patients and families face medical crises and their attendant decisions.

Because its aims are practical, and its theoretical ambitions quite modest, this discussion deals briefly or not at all with a large number of theoretical debates in the field of medical ethics. These issues are important, and they have significant moral, legal, and political implications. However, I have judged that discussing them in any depth would make this book too long and too far removed from pastoral practice to be much use to those to whom it is primarily addressed. Nonetheless, I am well aware, and the reader should also be aware, that some of the positions taken in this volume are a long way from uncontroversial. This is *a* version of the relation between medical ethics and Christian faith; I would be willing to make a more detailed argument for it, but I do not do so here. In this context I should note that the dedication to Dr. Margaret A. Farley, Gilbert L. Stark Professor of Christian Ethics at Yale Divinity School, expresses a long-standing debt to a wonderful teacher. It should not be taken to imply her agreement with either the methods or the conclusions of this volume.

Much of the material in this book was originally prepared for a two-day continuing education event for United Methodist pastors in the Baltimore area in April, 1994. I wish to thank that group of ministers for their enthusiastic participation, their questions, and the personal conversations and story-telling that surrounded our more formal sessions. I hope a more complete and detailed written presentation of those reflections will be as useful to them, and others like them, as their comments and reactions were to me.

Because a book like this is intended not for academics but primarily for ministers and other care givers, I have relied substantially on the responses and suggestions of friends and colleagues with experience in pastoral and clinical settings. In particular I want to thank Rev. Michael Armstrong, Rev. David McAllister-Wilson, and Rev. Verlee North-Shea for their comments and advice. As they will see, I have benefited from their insights.

As in everything I do, my husband, Tom, has been an active partner in this work from the beginning, serving as text editor, debate partner, critic, and provider of moral and material support of all kinds. All practical help aside, without his affection and encouragement I would never have the heart to undertake such tasks, much less complete them. Finally, my children, Sarah, Jessica, and Timothy, provide me with continual reminders of the sweetness and the seriousness of caring for the people who are entrusted to us, but who never belong to us.

Introduction

Playing God or Struggling to Be Human? Bioethics and Christian Faith

Occasionally when I lecture to seminary students or lay church groups on areas of bioethics[1] such as the criteria for terminating life-support or for decisions not to treat, someone asks me if I do not think of this whole area as an example of "playing God." I have a great deal of sympathy for that question, and for the moral and theological perspective it represents.

How do we dare to make such decisions? How can we presume to know that a life has reached its limit, or that the obligations of doctors and nurses to provide treatment to the sick are ended in a particular case? What gives us the confidence in our own judgment, hampered by ignorance and distorted by sin, to make and carry out a plan not to attempt resuscitation on a patient when we know that we might be able to restart heartbeat and breath?

Part of the answer is that nothing can give us unqualified confidence in such matters. Whenever I am teaching students who will function in their professional lives as care givers or as hospital chaplains, I tell them that anyone who is not sometimes kept up at night anguishing over such decisions does not understand what he or she is doing. And anyone who is unable to face the fact that, some of the time, our best and most conscientious judgments will be wrong, had better find another line of work.

But the other part of the answer, and the only thing that can justify the enterprise of medical ethics, is that such decisions cannot be avoided. We are making them all the time, one way or another, overtly or covertly, well or badly, and we cannot escape doing so. We are making them because the practice of medicine itself, and the business of treatment, *is* a human intervention, an action calculated to bring about a certain result we see as desirable. Whenever we seek or provide medical care—antibiotics, insulin, radiation, or the bodily invasion we call surgery—we are already departing from the policy of "letting nature take its course." Thus, we are making a decision when we initiate treatment, and we are making new decisions every moment as we actively continue it.

No one who has been present at a full-scale resuscitation effort can miss the active, decisive, even violent character of that intervention. People run, they shove needles into veins, they shout to the team to stand clear, and they send 200 volts of electricity through the heart while forcing oxygen into and out of the lungs. We speak of an order *not* to resuscitate because that is a departure from ordinary practice, but we ought to speak as well of an order *to* resuscitate, or of a standing policy to do so, and recognize it for what it is: a full scale assault upon death itself, an apparent effort to wrest the decisive moment from the province of nature, and some have argued, from the province of God as well.

It has been held by groups such as Christian Scientists that medicine is in fact just such a prideful assault upon divine providence, and that it manifests an inadequate trust in God's care. The majority Christian view, of which I am a part, sees the exercise of scientific and clinical skill to treat the sick as part of the human task of care and stewardship. On this view, the cultivation of human knowledge and human powers to intervene in disease is part and parcel of the mandate to exercise "dominion" over creation, and an aspect of our obligation to share the necessities of ordinary life, which include health care, with those in need. But recognizing that any medical act or omission is a *human* decision, and a decision which can have consequences of great weight, means that we are never free of the burden of medical decision-making. Likewise, we are never free of the task of clarifying and defending and reviewing the choices we *do* make, whether they are choices to initiate treatment or to withdraw it, or choices between alternative courses of treatment.

But the making of such choices cannot be merely a private matter, an expression of personal taste and opinion, where an individual practitioner or an individual patient simply calls the shots in sovereign independence. The resources of medicine are *social* resources, from research grants to the physical structures that house medical education to the physical, donated bodies upon which that education and research depend. The practice of medicine is a *social* practice, part of an ethos of common life which expresses the basic convictions of a society, and the values and judgments that flow from them. Therefore we need to think long and hard, together and out loud, about the aims of medicine and the acts that accord with them: about the scope and the limits of our responsibility for one another; about the meaning and the shape of care for mortal bodies and the persons who, for lack of language more precise, live in and through them. For all these reasons, bioethics is an inescapable part of the task of being human, part of the burden and privilege of moral freedom.

But I want to argue here that it is also part of the task of being Christian. This is partly because, as I have already suggested, the provision of medical care is a natural extension of our commanded responsibility to share "the things needed by the body" (James 2:16) with those in need. Decisions about what kind of care we give to whom and under what circumstances cannot be foreign to Christian moral reflection. On this ground alone, health care reform and ensuring access to health care for our most vulnerable populations are *theological* issues. But also and more centrally, bioethics is a task for the church because the questions it is constrained to ask and answer are *theological* questions, at least from the standpoint of any believer. Some examples will serve to make the point clear.

Questions about whether to offer artificial life-support in a particular case are implicitly questions about why we support human life: For the sake of what? In difficult cases, the particular decisions cannot be made intelligibly or defended cogently apart from some account of why human life has a distinctive sort of moral claim upon us. Related questions concern the meaning and value of bodily function itself: Do the basic functions of heartbeat and circulation, respiration and metabolism have moral importance in and of themselves, such that they are to be extended for as long as possible? Or are they supported for the sake of some other human functions or capacities, like consciousness or relationship or mental and physical activity? Should support for bodily functions be terminated when they no longer contribute to these ends? What ends are determinative? How do we know?

Correspondingly, questions about when to terminate treatment cannot be separated from questions about the purpose and ends of life, and the point at which they are fulfilled. They are the specification of more general questions about the limits of human power and responsibility for life, and about the content of human care and fidelity. From another angle, they are at the deepest level questions about the nature and foundation of hope and resignation for mortal beings. Questions about ending treatment are questions about the contingency of human life and the meaning of mortality. They are inescapably and sometimes agonizingly questions about the use and meaning of it all: questions about whether life in all its fragility and grief is a good gift after all. Finally, in their individual human forms, at the bedside of the sick and dying and standing with those who love them, they are questions about where God is when you need God, and about how we know.

But bioethics is not a theological enterprise only when it is wrestling with life-and-death decisions about the treatment of individual patients. In considerations of what care is provided to whom and who pays for it, bioethics asks questions about who counts as a member of the community, and what are the conditions for membership. In attempting to answer such questions, it implies a theory about the relationships in which human beings live, and the moral meaning of their biological and social interdependence.

In addressing questions about who should receive the single transplantable organ which several patients need, bioethics asks and answers questions about the shape of justice in human society, an area that the prophets and epistle writers persist in viewing as a theological matter. In policy questions about who makes treatment decisions for minors or for those whose ability to make decisions is reduced or absent, we deal with the nature of the relation between self and body, and self and community, and with the nature of human liberty and obligation in dealing with the gift of the body.

This small sampling is large enough to explain my claim that, if central Christian convictions—that God is the Creator and Redeemer and Sustainer of life, and the One toward whom all life is directed as end and fulfillment—are true, then almost every serious decision about the treatment of the sick has theological implications. Individualism or community context, personal project or vocation and service, social contribution or being-in-relation to God and each other: these construals of the situation and the meaning of human existence are implicit in our language and our reflection about medical care, and in turn they are enacted and given authority by the decisions we make and the policies we embrace.

As theologians, as pastors, and as Christians, we have a great deal at stake in making these decisions prayerfully and responsibly, in a way that is consistent with our faith and congruent with our own distinctive account of the meaning and the end of human existence. The context needed to sustain the conversation that will help us to make such choices well in a crisis is the community of faith. Partly this is because here we are among those who share our specific moral convictions and commitments. But more than that, it is because it is here that we are formed into the persons that we are, here that our vision of the world and our understanding of the choices we confront is deeply shaped by the story of God we tell, and by the experiences we share. And in any deeply frightening and wrenching decision, the clarity and the balance we need to see truthfully and to choose well can only be attained within a community that shares such a story, and the character that story forms over time.

For all these reasons, Christian ministers need to be prepared to lead their parishioners and their communities in a process of discernment about how we are to care for the sick and the dying. They can do so not as those who have mastered the "answers" to uncertainty and conflict and grief, but as those who are able to withstand the questions, and to create the space in which Christians can face the questions squarely in the light of their common convictions, and their shared trust in God's ultimate mercy.

Accordingly, we will begin in Chapter 1 by exploring the distinctive character and shape of Christian ethics as they are visible in the Scriptures of the Christian community. This will provide our starting point as we consider why Christians should particularly care about medicine as a moral practice, and what insights and questions our faith teaches us to bring to its coordinate task of ethical analysis and justification.

In Chapter 2, we will go on to consider the meaning and the use of the four standard principles of obligation in bioethics: autonomy, non-maleficence, beneficence, and justice. Particularly we will look at what happens to them if they are placed in the context of, and sometimes in tension with, Christian convictions and Christian understandings of the task of moral life. In proceeding in this fashion, we are to some extent bowing to the moral methodology common in the field of medical ethics, where argument typically proceeds from these or similar principles (variously understood and supported) to justify particular actions in given situations. The fact is that most pastors and most of their parishioners will confront these issues in the context of someone being cared for in a health care setting where this paradigm and its methods are taken for granted. Therefore, pastors must be conversant with this language and competent in its use.

However, there is another reason for our being engaged, albeit critically, with this language of principles and their application; it is the way in which the languages of narrative, virtue, and principle relate to and even depend upon one another. On one hand, as the earlier examples suggest, the standard method of moral analysis in bioethics is not nearly as "neutral" or objective as its employment in secular and pluralistic contexts makes it appear. The substantive meanings of qualities like justice or beneficence must be constructed: they are hardly evident in the terms themselves. An account of rationality, so crucial to any appeal to the principle of autonomy, turns out to depend on a prior account of reality, just as an understanding of the goods and harms weighed in judging beneficence or maleficence depends upon a prior understanding of human well-being and fulfillment—in fact on an anthropology, or a theology. Therefore, the notion of universal, belief-neutral principles which have only to be applied to new situations to yield moral clarity is itself illusory.

Conversely, even when we have a distinctively Christian understanding of moral life as the human response to God's acts set forth in Scripture, or as centrally concerned with the transformation of believers' character into the likeness of Jesus Christ, we necessarily employ what might be called "mediating structures." For example, in moving from the imitation of Christ in the virtue of fidelity to the concrete acts and forbearances of caring for the sick, we will of necessity select, order, interpret, and summarize both the biblical witness and the situation on which we bring that witness to bear. We will identify some events and some motifs in the narrative as crucial or paradigmatic. (One can see this process at work in even the earliest creeds.) We will also, in conversation with the Scriptures and with the Christian tradition, give some content to the virtues which are to be formed, and to the kinds of behavior to which those virtues dispose us.

One way to express the conduct which flows from our stories and from our account of the morally good life is through the formulation of general moral norms. This is hardly a modern phenomenon, or one wholly alien to Christian moral instruction. Obviously there is the body of Torah, which includes according to Orthodox Jewish scholars 613 positive and negative commandments. But the same Paul who described the heart of Christian morality as "do not be conformed to this world, but be transformed by the renewing of your minds" (Rom. 12:2) did not hesitate to formulate principles as general as "as far as possible, do good to all persons" (Gal. 6:10). Even the command "love your neighbor" has the formal character of a principle, the expression of a general moral duty. Like other paradigms of moral thought—command-obedience, law-compliance, ends-means, virtue-formation—the paradigm of general principle-concrete application is an inadequate vehicle for conveying the power and richness of Christian moral life and reflection. It remains, nonetheless, one of the tools by which we order and communicate a broader and deeper moral wisdom, and one which can be used well or badly. We have some stake in using it as well as we can.

Other aspects of the methodological distinctiveness of medical ethics as a theological task—such as the role of the community, the constraints upon Christian understandings of suffering, and the centrality of prayer—will become clear in later chapters. There we will talk about use of bioethical principles to illuminate difficult cases (Chapter 3) and the role of the minister in addressing questions of medical ethics (Chapter 4). Finally, we will grapple with the limits of this and all efforts at human care and human insight.

Chapter 1

Christian Faith, Ethics, and the Moral Practice of Medicine

Like any book in the field of Christian ethics, this one is written from a particular point of view. That is true not only in the particular positions it takes on the issues it discusses, but more fundamentally in its assumptions about the possibility and the character of Christian ethics. It is not self-evident, nor is it universally agreed, that there can *be* a distinctively Christian ethics; much less is there universal consensus about what might be the starting point of such an ethic (assuming it exists), or how it might proceed. An extensive discussion of various possible understandings of the nature of Christian ethics is beyond the scope of this book. Still, it is important to be clear from the outset about what I take to be the place of moral reflection and moral self-criticism in Christian life, and what kinds of language and what ways of thinking seem to me to belong to that enterprise.

Why Ethics Is a Bad Place to Start

The first thing to say about the disciplines of morality, whether conceptual or practical, is that they are the wrong place to *begin* thinking about Christian faith and Christian life. Despite the prevalence of this way of thinking and talking in our culture, the Christian community is *not* defined by those who behave in some particular way, any particular way, and it is not composed of those who engage in the behavior we call "going to church." Nor is it made up of those who hold some particular moral opinion or group of them, whether these be convictions about abortion or about violence or about the family or about any of a range of other serious and important issues.

Instead, the Christian church consists of those people who believe the things that Christians affirm, which are in the first instance not moral statements at all. Whether one thinks of these affirmations in the declaratory form found in the historic creeds ("I believe in God, Creator of heaven and earth . . .") or in the narrative form they take in Scripture ("In the beginning, God made the heavens and the earth . . ."), they are in the first place affirmations about what God has done, not about what we must do.

To be sure, both creeds and Scripture go on to call upon those making the affirmations for some kind of response. The creeds do this indirectly in the form of affirming the holiness of the church, the guidance of the Spirit, and the practices of forgiveness and of baptism. Scripture for its part gives a richly developed and sometimes quite specific account of the appropriate human response to God's gracious acts. But two things are crucial. The first is that, in both venues, it is overwhelmingly the recital of God's acts that takes center stage. The second is that the human response called for centrally takes the form of entering into certain sorts of relationships, rather than of acting according to certain dictates.

The concrete obligations of Torah have as their center and purpose the invitation to be God's people, as the commands of Jesus can be gathered into the one call, "be my disciples." Analogously, what the creeds call for is the entrance through baptism and forgiveness into the "communion of the saints," reaching through time and space to embrace all who take its story of creation, redemption, and consummation as their own. To put it somewhat differently, the kind of "believing" that is in question, the kind that does not merely characterize but constitutes the church, includes both intellectual assent and personal commitment. The "faith" in view is much more than giving credence; it is giving oneself to the God who is believed, and into the community created by what God in Jesus Christ has done for all in common.

But if Christian faith begins with what God has done, and with the relationships into which we are invited as our response, it cannot end there. To be a disciple is to have a master. On one hand, it is the prior relationship with Christ and the desire to respond to him in gratitude that gives Christian significance to our conduct. On the other, our relationship with Christ as Lord must be brought to life in character and conduct if it is to have any reality. Thus, the community of faith is a moral community—a community of mutual discipline and mutual accountability—not incidentally, but *essentially*. Ethics is not the starting point of Christian faith, and morality is not its heart—but neither is the call to "live a life worthy of the gospel" merely optional. It is clear in both the New Testament and the broad Christian tradition that it is for the sake of the transforming power of this community, as well as for the sake of witness, that the church exists. Indeed, the transformed life of the community and its ability to bear witness to the gospel cannot be separated.

Given this understanding of Christian ethics as a response to God's grace, as derivative without being dispensable, what language and what ways of understanding moral life make sense? What is it we are trying to do, and what shape should the task of moral reflection and discernment take? Especially, how ought we to think about the ethical issues of medicine in light of Christian convictions? Because in the view here presented it is the biblical story which forms the church, we must begin with at least a schematic account of that narrative.

God's Story and Christian Character

This story of what God has done provides the framework within which Christians interpret the world and their acts in it. It is only because we read this as our own story that we can receive the gospel of Jesus Christ as the resolution of the crisis of our alienation, and the foundation of a new way of living in the world. At the same time, the practices of remembering and retelling the story actively shape the community, because just as the story *fosters* a certain moral character, it also *requires* a certain character. Who can habitually tell a story which depicts her as the undeserving recipient of a kindness she can never merit without first giving up hope of being vindicated on the world's terms? Christian character, then, is both that formed by the story we tell, and that which enables us to tell the story rightly.[1]

The narrative of Scripture reaches in a long arc from the scene of creation in the garden, ending with the loss of communion with God and exile from the Tree of Life, to the scene of re-creation climaxed by the descent of the New Jerusalem. There the Tree of Life blooms now in the midst of the city, and "the leaves of the tree are for the healing of the nations" (Rev. 22:2). In between, God calls Israel into being: there begins the long and often brutal drama of that relationship, with its many setbacks and catastrophes. The story of Israel climaxes with the prophetic promise, delivered on the eve of exile, of the Messiah who will come to bring the covenant with God's people to fruition.

The Gospels and Acts take up the narrative with the coming and the vindication of Jesus of Nazareth as that Messiah. They follow the course of his teaching and ministry ending with his death, and relate the story of the followers who haltingly came to believe and proclaim his resurrection and eventual return. The collection of letters to various churches provides us with a picture of the developing life and thought of those followers, as they begin trying to make sense of what has happened in the light of God's steady intention to restore God's creation. In the letters, the Apostles articulate how the death and resurrection of Christ has reconciled human beings to God, and made possible a new life in the world in light of the triumph of God's grace. Here as well the writers call upon the community of faith to embody the relations of trust, care and mutual dependence which God has made possible; this is to be their witness to the truth of the gospel and to its final fulfillment in the coming Kingdom.

Even so broad a sketch as this teaches us to see ourselves and our lives in quite distinctive and significant ways. Initially, we discover ourselves as creatures—that is as finite and wholly contingent, and yet the object of the divine will and love: made according to God's good pleasure, and given both a calling to cooperate with God's creative work and an invitation to a free and loving union with our Creator. Almost in the same breath, we discover ourselves as sinners, rebelling in ignorance and arrogance against the very gift of our being, seeking to be our own gods and to set the terms of our existence without constraint.

In this story we also discover God as Lover and Pursuer, as God—by turns in wrath, in sorrow, and in tenderness—seeks to check the spreading effects of sin in the world and provide a footing to reestablish the divine-human relationship, thus making possible the flourishing of all of creation. In the course of the narrative we gain an understanding of suffering as the manifestation of a world laboring under its own rebellion and delusion. We come to recognize suffering as real and significant without being final, and as an evil that God can yet make good and turn to God's own purpose of redemption. More particularly, in light of our present concerns, we come to see that our experience of the conditions of embodiedness and dependence as burdens rather than gifts is the result of our failure to trust in the goodness and faithfulness of God. More than anything else, we come to see ourselves as beloved and claimed, embraced by God's love and power, and to understand that, even in the midst of pain, grief and confusion, we are never abandoned.

To believe this story is to see that our ultimate well-being is beyond our ability to grasp, but also that it is wholly secure in what God has done and will yet do, in bringing us to the friendship with God and each other for which we were made. To believe this story, or better, to dwell within this story, is not to entertain illusions that the world is safe or benign, or to suppose that God will somehow shield us from evil and accident. It is rather to believe and be comforted by the affirmation, "neither death, nor life, nor angels, nor rulers, nor things present, nor things to come, nor powers, nor height, nor depth, nor anything else in all creation, will be able to separate us from the love of God in Christ Jesus our Lord" (Rom. 8:38-39).

The Correlative Virtues

What qualities and characteristics, what habits of mind and what dispositions to action would we expect to see in a community formed and sustained by such a story? In particular, how would a people formed by this story and disciplined by remembering and retelling it understand, undertake and respond to the task of caring for the sick and the dying? Initially, I will talk about the character and habits arising from the general shape of the narrative as outlined: responses to basic Christian convictions about the nature of human life as a gift and a trust, and to human well-being as secured by and in God and within the community of faith. Later on, I will look at the various kinds of explicitly moral conversation within the New Testament,[2] examining both its content and the kinds of reasoning it employs. In all these areas, I will be speaking not descriptively but normatively; that is, I am seeking not to describe the actual character and conduct of believers past or present, but rather to picture the character which accords with and lives out the faith they profess.

Perhaps the first point to make is that a community steeped in this account would understand the task of caring for the sick as both natural and obligatory. Seeing all human beings as the creatures of God compels one to recognize them as in essential respects the same as oneself, in that they are objects of the same divine care and call. The fact that they exist is sufficient sign that they are the recipients of God's grace and the objects of God's call to communion. Having thus the same source and the same destiny, human beings are connected to each other by their common relationship with their Creator. As the child of a friend is cherished for the sake of the love one bears the friend, so we may suppose that those who love the God who creates and sustains all persons will cherish and care for them for the sake of their divine Parent. Initially, then, we will look for an active compassion extending to all persons.

But to be a creature is also to be bound in time and space—to be finite, contingent, and mortal. Part of what we have in common with all persons is our vulnerability to injury, illness, and ultimately to death. A community schooled in accepting the limits of creatureliness, and sustained in hope by the trustworthiness of the Creator, has less reason than most to deny this fact. Unlike the prevailing culture, which must deny death at all costs since it shares no account of a good more fundamental than survival, Christian communities live in the belief that life is directed toward and fulfilled in the knowledge and love of God, goods which cannot be thwarted by death. These convictions can enable a kind of courage and even cheerfulness in the face of death that does not depend on the pretense of personal invulnerability. Thus, Christians need not flee from the intimations of our own mortality which are inevitably borne by the sick and the dying. We will look, therefore, for a greater readiness to be with, and to be truthful with, the sick and those facing death.

But if death is not an absolute terror, neither is life an absolute end. No community constituted by the belief that Christ has accepted death for the sake of our redemption can view life as a good which trumps all others, for the sake of which anything might be done. To begin with, life is seen as a gift rather than a possession or an entitlement,[3] and further its "value" is only instrumental. It is simply the venue of service, only the context in which to fulfill God's will—a will which certainly, at some point, embraces our dying.

Thus Paul is being neither hyperbolic nor heroic when he discusses with such detachment the odds of his surviving to visit in person the church at Philippi. He is simply reasoning from his own understanding of the status of a life already given over to God: "For me to live is

Christ, and to die is gain. If I am to go on living in the flesh, this will mean fruitful labor for me. . . . I desire to depart and be with Christ, which is better by far, but it is more necessary that I remain in the flesh for your sake" (Phil. 1:21-24, AT). Paul is quite well aware that neither his life nor his moral exhortation make any sense whatever unless his expectation of a destiny greater than life or death is vindicated: "If only for this life have we hoped in Christ, then we are of all people most to be pitied" (1 Cor. 15:19).

This has important implications for the ways in which Christians might understand the aims of health care. If it is not only impossible but in some sense unnecessary to stave off death forever, then medicine is freed from the futile and distorting goal of sustaining life indefinitely. Instead, it can be directed toward the larger good of supporting human well-being, and the related goods of care, fidelity and presence with people in their suffering and its loneliness. We will look for a distinctive account of the ends of medicine growing from a Christian account of what makes a worthwhile life.

A story whose most basic theme is redemption presupposes that the human situation is compromised and ambiguous. To put it more bluntly, the central Christian claim that we have a Savior is based upon the prior supposition that we are lost and need saving. In requiring us to recognize and represent ourselves as sinners, the gospel we proclaim continually reminds us that our perceptions, judgments, motives, and actions are distorted by falsehood and self-deception. The point here is not guilt or self-hatred, but readiness to be confronted and corrected by the claims and the arguments of others. A certain degree of self-suspicion, along with the remembrance that even our virtue is always partial and incomplete, disposes us to humility and patience with one another. (This is not inconsiderable; the standard complaint about medical practitioners is that they are arrogant and aloof, pretending to a certainty and an authority that place them above question or reproach.) More particularly, an acceptance of the "already but not yet" character of existence between redemption and consummation equips us to live with uncertainty and fallibility—our own and everyone else's. These qualities are essential if we are going to learn to make and to make sense of judgments in the world of medical practice, where decisions are relentlessly "right now," and results are always in the projected and unknowable future.

Perhaps no aspect of the Christian story or of the way of life that it entails seems more puzzling in the modern world than its focus on the community. Although there are memorable and richly portrayed individuals within the narrative, even in their cases it is the connection to a larger community of faith that makes them worthy of attention. Abraham, patriarch of the Jews and exemplar of saving faith to the Gentiles, is remembered precisely as the father of Israel and the prototype of the church's faith. Peter, most impetuous and individual of the disciples, is singled out because his is the faith which founds the church. Even Christ himself, for all his uniqueness, is praised as "the firstborn from the dead," and thus the forerunner of all the redeemed. From the first rupture in the peace of creation, God's strategy for restoration has been the calling into being of a community which could preserve and embody the truth of God's gracious reign.

The story we tell of God's dealing with human beings teaches us to understand a human life in terms of its place in a community and its relation to other lives. In fact, so powerful is the corporate model of the church's existence in Scripture that it is only as a member of and contributor to the body of Christ that a Christian life *has* a moral character. Such an understanding provides a new set of questions and a broader set of resources for thinking through issues in medical care. To begin to fill in the discussion of how a community focus might affect moral conversation and reflection about care of the sick, we must turn to particular texts. This we will begin to do in the next section, where we look at some of the actual moral instruction of the New Testament, and especially at how it justifies the conduct it recommends.

Moral Conversation in the New Testament

In one sense it is quite easy to answer a question such as "What does the Bible say about withdrawing life support?" because the Bible says nothing whatever about the matter. The conditions that make it both possible and necessary to ask the question had not yet arisen. The same is true of most of the specific "problems" of medical ethics, since they generally amount to questions about how (and whether) we should use medical techniques and technologies which have come into existence only in the last four or five decades. Even questions of medical ethics which were in existence and had been part of moral conversation for hundreds of years before the writing of the New Testament—the duties of the physician, how much truth to tell the sick, etc.—do not come into the canon as matters of explicit concern.

It is only as we look at the assumptions and the questions which lie behind our ethical problems that we find the actual moral teaching of the New Testament helpful or relevant. For it is perfectly explicit about matters like who counts as an object of concern, what we owe to one another, and what the motives and goals of our choices ought to be. It is to the Bible's shaping of these basic assumptions, its formation of the vision which forms the moral horizons of our lives and the context of all our decisions, that we now turn. Of course, moral teaching in Scripture is not always presented propositionally, in the form of principles to apply or imperatives to obey (although there is plenty of that kind of instruction). It often takes the forms of parable and prayer, of oracle and historical report, of example and exhortation and ecstatic vision, as well as that of outright instruction.

It is not my intention here to recite every such "lesson" that might be relevant to our caring for the sick; indeed that way of thinking of it does not do justice to the deep and pervasive way in which the ethos of the community is shaped by its use of Scripture. Instead, I will raise a few central and representative topics (the community context of morality, the centrality of love, the theme of the imitation of God, the understanding of suffering) and look at some of the passages which might shape our thinking about them. These can be no more than examples, crucial strokes on a much broader canvas. They serve mainly to call to our attention recurrent patterns or motifs in the moral language of the New Testament. And in all cases, we will be as interested in how the writers think, argue and persuade as in what they commend or prohibit. At this point we are not so much trying to solve our problems about treating the sick as we are trying to see how, as Christians, we ought to begin thinking about them.

Community Context

As already indicated, one of the most distinctive aspects of moral thinking in the New Testament is its focus on the community of believers. The community of faith provides both the context and the rationale for moral reflection and judgment. This means that Christians turn to one another for counsel and insight, and are accountable to one another for the coherence of their conduct and their profession. But it also means that one of the primary ways in which behavior is judged is by its contribution to the well-being and growth of the community.

Paul characteristically encourages the churches to think through "disputable matters" (Rom. 14:1, NIV) not in terms of what behavior is lawful or even right but what conduct is "edifying": literally, what "builds up" the community. This is especially apparent in his discussions of what was evidently a pressing issue of his day, whether Christians should eat meat which has been ritually offered to idols (1 Cor. 8:1-13; 10:14-33). The same concern animates his discussion of food regulations and feast days in Romans 14:1-23. The conclusion which is to be applied to such matters he gives there:

> If your brother or sister is being injured by what you eat you are no longer walking in love. . . . Let us then pursue what leads to peace and to mutual upbuilding. Do not, for the sake of food, destroy the work of God. Everything is indeed clean, but it is wrong for you to make others fall by what you eat. (Rom. 14:15, 19-20)

Paul's strategy is to shift the focus of the conversation from "Who is right?" to "What will unite the community?" His effort is to protect not the correct opinion, but the community's weakest members. This suggests ways of dealing with moral disagreements among Christians or even among different religious groups. It gives us a more substantial reason than a vapid tolerance for respecting scruples we do not share; we do so in order not to wound conscience in its effort to keep faith with God.

This is perhaps a better way of understanding why, for example, it is important not to compel adult Jehovah's Witnesses to receive critically needed blood transfusions. At present we tend to allow such refusals with an air of great condescension, under the heading of people being entitled to hold whatever crazy opinions they like. On Paul's model, we might take such a refusal quite seriously as an evidence of the desire to please God, and honor that moral seriousness even if we find the prohibition itself wholly misguided. Paul wisely cautions against the temptations on both sides of such debates. To those who refrain from disputed practices he warns, "You must not condemn the one who does [eat]. . . . . Who are you to judge another's servant?" (Rom. 14:3-4, AT). And of the enlightened and liberal he inquires, "Why do despise your brother or sister? . . . For we will all stand before God's judgment seat" (Rom. 14:10, AT).

Love, the Touchstone

It would be a mistake to conclude from this that all matters of Christian behavior are, like food regulations, indifferent in themselves. Paul in these letters and elsewhere is perfectly ready to declare some acts simply incompatible with Christian faith and life. He writes to the Corinthians, for example, that they are not to associate with anyone "who bears the name of brother" if he is immoral or greedy or an idolater or a thief (1 Cor. 5:11). But for Paul, even these prohibitions are no more than concrete specifications of the duty of love which both marks and sustains the community of faith:

> The commandments, "You shall not commit adultery; You shall not murder; You shall not steal; You shall not covet"; and any other commandment, are summed up in this word, "Love your neighbor as yourself." Love does no wrong to a neighbor; therefore, love is the fulfilling of the law. (Rom. 13:9-10)

We must show regard for each others' scruples even when they are in error, must be focused less on our prerogatives than on mutual nurture, because love is both wellspring and hallmark of Christ's own life which is being formed among us. In later developments of the Pauline tradition, love is the bond which unites the body whose growth and life is the church: "we must grow up in every way into [Christ] who is the head, from whom the whole body . . . builds itself up in love" (Eph. 4:15-16, AT). Thus, the readiness to "please others rather than ourselves," in Paul's repeated phrase, is our imitation of and testimony to Christ, who has become a servant for our sake and left us permanently owing the "debt" (Rom. 13:8) of love. Paul ends his long discussion on mutual forbearance in Romans 14 and 15 with the admonition, "Welcome one another, therefore, just as Christ has welcomed you, for the glory of God" (15:7).

The writer of 1 John goes even further. He does not hesitate to make the presence of an active and practical love within the Christian community the test for the truth of its claim to have received God's grace: "We know that we have passed from death to life because we love one another. Whoever does not love abides in death" (1 John 3:14). Here too the love to be practiced within the community is grounded in the imitation of God's own nature: "The one who does not love does not know God, *because* God is love" (4:8, AT).

It seems to the author of 1 John quite impossible that those who have been visited and transformed by the love of God, whose lives are lived in daily dependence upon and celebration of that love, could fail to embody it in their treatment of one another. And there is nothing mystical or vague or sentimental about the love the writer has in mind; he is talking not about warm feelings but about practical commitment:

> By this we know what love is: [Jesus Christ] laid down his life for us, and we ought to be willing to lay down our lives for our brothers and sisters. Whoever has the goods of this world and sees his brother in need but has no pity on him, how can the love of God be in him? Beloved, let us love not in words on the tongue, but in deed and in truth. (1 John 3:16-18, AT)

Love—understood as a vigorous, practical, and sacrificial devotion to the welfare of sisters and brothers—makes the weak and general duty of beneficence, central to most accounts of the obligations of medicine, seem quite pale by comparison. To take such a norm seriously would transform how we understood our obligations to the sick. It could, for example, shift the balance of the present debate about the extent of a health care provider's duty to treat dangerous infectious diseases. It might also have implications for how we understand patients' well-being, and what might count for someone as a rational choice about treatment. A parent or a sibling might for the sake of such a love make a decision which looks "irrational" because it risks substantial or even fatal harm to the decision-maker.

An example recently made the local newspapers in which a woman was diagnosed with uterine cancer early in a long-awaited pregnancy. She refused the recommended abortion and radiation therapy, and was delivered of a healthy daughter shortly before her death. There are many things to say about such a tragedy, including raising the serious objection that women in our society continue disproportionately to bear the burdens of such a love; this is not a kind of fidelity that may be recommended by the powerful for the powerless. But even that kind of social analysis cannot displace the centrality or the costliness of love in Christian moral life. To live such a life, or even to suffer such a death, is to imitate and to share in the very life of God in the world.

Imitation

I have already shown how Paul and the writer of 1 John use the love and mercy of God and of Christ as a basis for shaping the character and conduct of Christians. Similarly, 1 Peter invokes Christ as the model and exemplar of holiness (1:15: "As he who called you is holy, be holy yourselves in all your conduct") and of patient endurance in suffering (2:21: "To this you were called, because Christ also suffered for you, leaving you an example"). The theme of moral life as based on the emulation of God's own character or of Christ's ministry toward us is woven as well throughout the Gospels. There it is used as the basis for defining and commanding the attitudes, dispositions and concrete actions appropriate to Jesus' followers.

In the Gospel of Mark, Jesus is the prototype of fidelity, and the whole of faithfulness can be summed up in "following" or imitating him. In the Sermons of Matthew 5–6 and Luke 11–12, Jesus calls on his disciples to imitate God in the practice of patient forgiveness ("seventy times seven") and impartiality ("God sends rain on the just and the unjust"). In the final scene before his entry into Jerusalem, and in the Passion narratives of Luke and John, Jesus presents himself as a model of humble service and of love evidenced by the readiness to be sacrificed, and explicitly directs the disciples to imitate him in their life together (Matt. 20:25-28; Luke 22:24-27; John 13:2-17; 15:12).

The aim of this imitation is multiple. Initially, it serves to call under judgment all of our own partial, limited and selective ideas of goodness: "If you love those who love you, what reward do you deserve? Don't the tax collectors do the same thing?" (Matt. 5:46, AT). In addition, insofar as the church embodies these virtues, it gives testimony to God's character, and makes credible its preaching about God's nature and God's work of establishing the church: "This is how everyone will know you are my disciples: if you love each other" (John 13:35, AT). Finally, our emulation of God is part of our restoration into the divine image in which and for which we were created. In its ultimate form, it demands what only God can accomplish: "Be perfect, therefore, as your heavenly Father is perfect" (Matt. 5:48).

Both the particular virtues we are to imitate, and the notion that God's own perfection is the final standard of conduct, have dramatic implications for how and why Christians should care for the sick. The demand that we love even enemies, just as God sustains both the good and the evil, effectively answers the question of who counts as a worthy recipient of medical care. This is a point explicitly underscored in the parable of the Good Samaritan, down to the concluding exhortation, "Go and do likewise" (Luke 10:30-37).

The idea that the hospitality we are to extend to each other is to be modeled on Christ's welcome of us (Rom. 15:8) speaks to the graciousness with which care is to be extended. The command to imitate Christ's humility in washing the disciples' feet requires that we be willing to attend to the mundane needs of others. Over all stands the fundamental demand that the character of our love be like the love which God has shown us: universal in its scope and unwavering in its faithfulness, willing to bear the costs of love in a fallen world. This is the fidelity which Christians celebrate and bear witness to, give thanks for and embody, in their care for the sick.

Suffering

I have already spoken briefly and generally about what the Christian story entails in its view of suffering: that it is real and morally significant; that it is a genuine evil, without being either final or ultimate in its devastation. Now, in this context of bearing the costs of love, it is time to look more closely at the meaning and the effect of suffering as part of a Christian life.

Whereas we tend to regard suffering as an anomaly or an offense, suffering in the New Testament is taken utterly for granted. It is hard to overstate how basic a difference this is between our own moral culture and that of the biblical writers. Partly this is a reflection of the very different life circumstances of first-century believers, which exposed the great majority to a physically more difficult and riskier existence. Most people would have lost family members to accident or illness, and even for the healthy the task of surviving entailed a great deal more labor and discomfort than we typically experience.[4] Apart from the general conditions of material existence, the New Testament was written in a political context of military occupation, and of sporadic persecution of Jewish and Christian minorities. The writers and readers of the New Testament had plenty of experience with pain, hardship, and grief.

But the attitude toward suffering in the New Testament is not just a historical accident. It is a theological posture grounded on the expectation that faithfulness to the Gospel might well be as costly for disciples as it had been for their Master. To acknowledge and live under the sole lordship of God in a world of tyrannies of every description is, after all, a dangerous occupation. The question was not whether one would suffer but how and why—what was worth suffering for, and how one might make sense of that suffering. It is the conviction that one might suffer for doing right—or that suffering might be bound up in well-doing—that lies behind most of the New Testament's discussion of suffering.

This expectation of innocent suffering is formed pre-eminently by the story of Jesus' own arrest, torture and execution. Of the twelve times that the Greek verb "suffer" (*paschó*) appears in the gospels, nine speak of the suffering of Jesus, and all are linked directly to his fulfillment of his role and mission as the Son of Man.[5] It is the story of Jesus' suffering, and the Christian claim that hidden in it is the "victory that overcomes the world," that permanently transforms the meaning of suffering for his followers. From being a presumed punishment for sin, or an evidence of abandonment by God, suffering becomes at once a sign of the world's deep alienation from God, and a means by which God can overcome alienation and redeem creation. It is his willingness to suffer that is the final testimony to Jesus' love for God and for us, and his capacity to bear suffering for the sake of that love which makes redemption possible.

It is of enormous importance that we not mistake the claim that God can vindicate and redeem suffering, wresting good out of its evil, for the claim that suffering is not evil. To say that God has wrought good out of the death of Jesus Christ (or the suffering of any other innocent) no more blesses or condones cruelty and oppression than a life-saving organ donation from a murder victim exonerates the murderer. To say that faithfulness may require us to suffer is not to seek it or to glorify it or to excuse those who inflict it needlessly. But it is the power to endure evil for the sake of good that makes possible goods which can otherwise never be achieved; in our own lives as in Jesus', it is the virtue of courage which makes faithfulness possible.

This may help to make sense of the New Testament's talk about the meaning and the fruit of suffering, and its effort to form Christians into people capable of accepting suffering for the sake of the life to which they are called. Repeatedly Christians are told they must be prepared to suffer with Christ and for the sake of his name, as a consequence of bearing witness to him (Acts 5:41; Rom. 8:14; Phil. 1:29; 1 Pet. 4:12-16). They are told not to be surprised or dismayed by these "trials," and not to suppose that they have been abandoned in them. In the midst of these sufferings they are even exhorted to rejoice, for in them their own faith is deepened and perfected: "suffering produces perseverance, and perseverance produces character, and character produces hope, and hope does not disappoint us, because God's love has been poured into our hearts by the Holy Spirit that has been given to us" (Rom. 5:3-5).

In one of the most extended and difficult texts on suffering, 1 Peter urges those suffering unjustly to bear the injustice patiently in imitation of Christ (2:19-21), and claims that their endurance may be the means by which others come to recognize the truth of the gospel (3:2). It is crucial to remember that the writer does identify the suffering which he addresses as *unjust*, and likens it to the crucifixion of Christ; this is hardly to condone those who inflict it. Moreover, though they are counseled to submit like Christ even to those who mistreat them, it is important to note that the women and slaves Peter here addresses are not to be cowed: in the face of threats they are "to do right and let nothing terrify them" (3:6). Above all, they are exhorted not to fear what suffering the world can inflict (1 Pet. 3:14-15; also Matt. 10:26, 28; Rev. 2:10), but to remain faithful and fear only God.

In sum, suffering is to be relieved where possible, and shared where it cannot be relieved, but always believers are to place their hope in the vindication of God who will comfort, heal, and redeem. "I consider that the sufferings of this present time are not worthy to be compared with the glory that will be revealed in us" (Rom. 8:18).

The expectation that suffering may be the price of love and faithfulness for Jesus' followers as it was for him casts some of the current debates in medical ethics in a different light. It brings into focus questions often evaded in discussions of what actions should be taken in order to end suffering: Whose suffering are we concerned to end? Is the current pressure to authorize active measures to end the lives of the chronically ill or the dying aimed to relieve *their* suffering, or *ours*, as we are forced to endure with them the limits of mortality and disease? Is the increased willingness to forgo treatment for handicapped newborns who are not terminally ill an expression of our care for them, or of our unwillingness to be with and care for the unbeautiful or the unproductive? These are questions which we must continue to ask ourselves as we wrestle with issues of social policy. Our tradition reminds us that we may not uncritically embrace an ethic which regards suffering as the worst of all evils, and so is prepared to end suffering by removing the sufferer if all else fails. Neither are we entitled to do anything whatever to avoid for ourselves the suffering that may be entailed by our fidelity to the sick, the dying, and the handicapped.

These considerations by no means foreclose the discussion, and there is nothing in Christian faith incompatible with the belief that we ought to end or prevent suffering if we can do so: quite the contrary. The issue is what we should be willing to do to achieve that end, and how we ought to understand and deal with that suffering which cannot rightly be avoided or eliminated. The relevance of such questions, and of all of the foregoing efforts to locate both moral life and ethical analysis within the framework of Christian convictions, will be evident as we move now into discussion of the classic principles of bioethics, and what Christians might make of them.

Chapter 2

The Language of Bioethics: Philosophical Principles and Christian Convictions

Bioethical Principles and Their Foundations

The word "principle" comes from a Latin root which means literally "source," and it is helpful to think of principles as expressions of broad obligations which provide the source or warrant for more particular duties or rules. In turn, principles themselves can be grounded in different ways. They can be understood as expressions of God's will, or as required by rational consistency, or as serving the general good, or a number of other possibilities. Most modern discussions of medical ethics which aim to be comprehensive are organized around four general principles or duties: *autonomy*, *non-maleficence*, *beneficence*, and *justice*.

The definitions and the implications of these principles in the literature of bioethics are drawn mostly from secular moral philosophers such as Immanuel Kant and John Stuart Mill (or to use contemporary examples, John Rawls and Peter Singer). Discussions in the field tend to be closely focused on the dilemmas of patient care or research, or at most on the nature of the relationship between physician and patient. They do not usually include direct and explicit talk about the nature of a human person, or what is distinctive and worthwhile about human life, questions which are thought to belong more to the area called "philosophical anthropology." Nevertheless, all fully developed explanations of the foundation and content of human moral obligations (i.e., all moral philosophies) either articulate or assume such an anthropology; they imply a picture of the nature of human beings and human life. Those assumptions are present under the surface in the very way in which secular moral language is constructed and used, even by those who intend to be neutral about questions as grand as the meaning of life.

For example, utilitarian moral theories follow John Stuart Mill in understanding the phrase "morally right" to mean "productive of the greatest good for the greatest number." According to this view, whatever produces the best outcome (i.e., the greatest good for the greatest number) is the right thing to do, and no other considerations enter in. There are a number of open questions left by such an account, most obviously, "How do we decide what constitutes someone's good?" and "How do we measure and compare goods?" But even before we begin to explore those issues, there is something more basic built into this way of thinking and talking. For what this language does is to understand human acts as isolated, always pointed into the future, and determined purely by the end in view. Also implicit in such language is a particular view of human beings: they are seen chiefly as individuals who operate upon situations to achieve their desired ends. There is no attention to history, or to the concrete relationships in which humans come into existence and live and make their choices. There is no sense of the past reaching forward into the action, either in the sense of forming the character of the actor or of shaping particular obligations such as those of promise-keeping or gratitude.

Of course, utilitarianism is not a morally empty theory, and the ends of morally praiseworthy action are not left open by it: they are "the greatest good of the greatest number" (although, as noted, there are controversies about what that good is, how we know and who gets to decide). But this way of framing moral questions assumes a certain sort of being as our hypothetical moral actor: someone who is fundamentally atomic, defined without reference to others; who acts upon logical calculation, like the "rational maximizer" presupposed in game theories, whose acts are completely determined by their foreseen effects in the future. And it assumes that this calculation of outcomes and the resultant choice of action is the primary stuff of moral life.

Now in fact there are pluses and minuses to this as to any account of the nature of human beings, and my point here is not particularly to attack the foundations of utilitarian moral theories. (Moreover, a similar analysis could easily be made of other kinds of moral language commonly used in bioethics.) What I want to do instead is draw attention to the great difference between assumptions like these on one hand, and those of, e.g., St. Paul, which I discussed in the preceding chapter.

For Paul, the crucial determinant of human moral existence is not our orientation toward the rational pursuit of future ends, but the decisive act of God in redeeming and reclaiming us and the world through the life, death and resurrection of Jesus Christ. We are thus to "live a life worthy of the gospel," to "grow up in every way into the image of the Lord Jesus," to act as "members of the Body of Christ," and a number of other things that have to do with remembering and declaring and being faithful to what God has already done in the past. We enter upon these tasks not as pure rational agents poised above possible courses of action, but as creatures of conflicting impulse, seeking to be freed from our captivity to sin. And the transformation we require is accomplished by the Holy Spirit, in and through the community of others similarly claimed and called by God's grace into the church. The primary task of moral life on this understanding is not decision-making, but communal embodiment of the gospel.

My intention is not to examine comparative anthropology at great length. It is simply to point out that the assumptions lying behind the ethical language we use have an effect on our moral reflection. It will be necessary to keep in mind the depth and the subtlety with which those assumptions operate in *all* moral languages, as we look both appreciatively and critically at the standard language and methods of bioethics.

In the pages that follow, I will define each of the principles of bioethics as plainly as possible. I will also look at some of the commonest applications of each of them in medicine, and at the problems, both theoretical and practical, that arise in those applications. I will try in each case to indicate the theological foundations that might lead Christians to embrace the duties expressed in these principles as their own. At the same time, I will lay out the limitations or necessary re-interpretations of these obligations that are introduced by the convictions that Christians share. What becomes of these principles and their application as we look at them, and at the quandaries they are to help us solve, through the lens of Christian faith?

Autonomy: Definition and Application

The principle of respect for autonomy protects the right (and responsibility) of every adult human being freely to make and act upon decisions regarding his or her own life and activities. It includes especially the right to have control over one's own person. Respecting autonomy, then, is giving due deference to this right, and it includes both creating the conditions for exercising choice, and supporting the fulfillment of what is chosen.

In medical contexts, respect for autonomy is most significantly expressed in the requirement of free and informed consent for medical procedures. In recent decades this requirement has become a matter of law as well as a matter of professional ethics and institutional policy, and in its legal and institutional form it has four distinct aspects. For informed consent to be given for treatment, there must be *disclosure*, *comprehension*, *voluntariness*, and *competence*.

Disclosure refers to the need to give the patient all the information needed to make an informed and intelligent decision about whether to agree to the proposed treatment. This includes information about the illness or injury for which treatment is required, its cause and its predictable progress or effects. It also includes information about the treatment being suggested, about its harmful as well as its beneficial effects, and how likely each of these is to occur. The patient must be told about alternative treatment possibilities, and about their corresponding risks and benefits. A person asked to consent to treatment must be told why her or his physician makes this recommendation, and what the consequences of refusing treatment are likely to be.

All of the foregoing sounds rather more straightforward than it is in practice. For one thing, it overlooks the degree to which diagnosis, prognosis, and the likely results of treatment are all matters of judgment rather than of simple fact. Although there are some conditions for which diagnostic tests are clear and decisive, there are many others for which competing interpretations might be offered. Even when diagnosis is certain, many conditions have quite unpredictable responses to treatment, and it is not clear how helpful a statistical account ("There is a 35% chance that chemotherapy will help") is to a patient trying to make a decision.

Beyond the uncertainties that are simply part of medicine, there are debates about just how much information a patient should receive. Should patients be warned of a 0.02% likelihood of a fatal allergic reaction to a diagnostic test when failing to get the test makes it significantly more likely that they will die of an undiagnosed problem? The present standard is that patients should be told everything a "reasonable person" would want to know to make the decision, leaving out possibilities so remote that it would not be rational to act based upon them. This is far from completely clear, but it is the best test yet devised for what should be disclosed in seeking consent for treatment.

Comprehension refers to the requirement that the patient understand the information she or he is given on which to base a decision about treatment. This requirement recognizes that the whole point of disclosure is defeated if the manner or the language in which the information is offered makes it impossible for the patient to understand what it means. Again, this is clearer in theory than in practice. It is easy to say that patients are not really informed if they do not understand what is told them; it is much more difficult to see how to help them understand what may be as complex as it is frightening, or even how to figure out what they do or do not understand. The kind and degree of difficulty depends upon the age, education, cultural background and situation of the patient and his or her family, and is often further complicated by language barriers between patients and their care givers.

The "state of the art" in this area is the provision of written material in the patient's native tongue which explains in clear and simple language the proposed treatment and its risks and benefits. To be effective, this must be gone over orally in some detail with patients and their families by a sympathetic nurse or physician, who can understand and answer questions and determine whether the proposed treatment is understood and consent is being given.

If disclosure and comprehension pertain to the "informed" aspect of consent, *voluntariness* pertains to its "free" aspect. Both treatment and the process by which consent for it is secured must be without coercion or constraint. Patients must not be made to feel that they will somehow be punished or abandoned if they refuse consent for a particular procedure, or be in any way frightened into accepting procedures they do not want to undergo. More subtly, providers must not be tempted to present their recommendations in such a way that patients feel they are being disloyal if they do not comply with the physician's prescribed course.

In his widely read book *How We Die*,[1] Dr. Sherwin Nuland tells of a 92-year-old patient to whom he recommended surgical repair of a life-threatening duodenal ulcer. The patient initially refused surgery, claiming that she had lived "quite long enough" (p. 251) and saw no need to undergo the pain and struggle of surgery and its aftermath when her general health was failing in any case. He recounts his successful effort to persuade her to have the operation, and her survival through surgery and a difficult recovery period, only to die a few weeks later from a massive stroke. He reveals as well his patient's sense of betrayal as she struggled through her post-operative ordeal in surgical intensive care.

In his unsparing self-reflections, Nuland accuses himself of "the worst sort of paternalism" (p. 252) because he deliberately misled the patient about how difficult recovery would be in order to secure her consent. But his account reveals as well another kind of paternalism, in that the patient tells him she is only yielding to his persuasion because of her personal trust in him. He recounts suddenly feeling "a little less sure I was doing the right thing" (p. 251). His misgivings are well founded, in that they signal the danger of exercising undue influence over a decision, making it more nearly the doctor's choice than the patient's. This can be particularly difficult to avoid when, as in this case, the physician's desire for the best outcome for the patient is mixed with his desire not to be "beaten" in the struggle to conquer disease. It is one of the times that different accounts of the goals of life and their fulfillment held by patients and their care givers may lead to very different ideas of what counts as a patient's benefit.

The final element of informed consent is *competence*. This refers to the mental and emotional ability of the patient to make free and reasonable choices about treatment. It includes cognitive assessments of the patient's ability to understand her situation and options. It also involves psychological judgments of sufficient maturity, rationality and emotional balance to permit reasoned reflection and choice. All conscious adult patients are presumed to be competent unless evidence to the contrary is presented. In that case, a court must make a judgment about competence similar to those it makes regarding the disposal of financial assets when a person is thought to be senile.

As one might expect from the use of words like "sufficient" and "reasoned," competence too is a matter of judgment, of degree, of the unquantifiable "more or less" of human abilities. How much cognitive ability is needed for competence? Can a retarded adult ever be judged competent to make treatment decisions? How much maturity is required? Can a 14-year-old cancer patient refuse chemotherapy? What counts as a reasoned judgment? Such questions could be multiplied. The difficulties of making judgments about competence are reflected in the lack of clear tests or criteria by which to make them.

A standard baseline for competence is given in the notation that a patient is or is not "oriented x 3." This refers to whether a conscious patient knows who she is, where she is, and what year it is. While it seems safe to say that these are necessary to justify a judgment of competence, they hardly seem sufficient grounds to do so. Sometimes patients are given psychological tests of various kinds, but these tests were designed to measure other kinds of cognitive or emotional functioning, and are not well suited for their new purpose. (For example, one common test originally designed to check for brain lesions involves counting backward from 100 by threes, a feat which has no particular relation to capacities for understanding and judgment.) The most sophisticated discussions of competence recognize that competence exists in various degrees, rather than being a simple attribute which one either has or lacks. They require higher levels of competence (such as the ability to describe the situation and give reasons for one's choices in it) when the risks or the burdens of a proposed treatment are greater.

We have now considered all of the elements of informed consent as it is understood in bioethics. But the principle of respect for autonomy has broader applications than the claim that patients have the right to give or withhold consent for treatment. Autonomy is also the basis of physicians' duty of confidentiality, as patients' rights to control the disclosure of personal information is seen as an aspect of control over their own lives. This is another form of the protective function of respect for autonomy, its operation as a barrier against a different form of invasion or assault.

But autonomy may also be construed as a positive claim, as an active right to do what you wish as long as it does not directly attack another. Some have used it to argue that patients have a broad right to medical cooperation or assistance in achieving a variety of personal goals or desires. It has been thought to give a foundation for patients' demand for access to experimental or untested therapies, or for forms of treatment thought to be futile in a particular case. Autonomy has also been the ground on which some have argued for a right to assistance (in the form of technical expertise, or of donor sperm or eggs, or of surrogate wombs) in obtaining a healthy, biologically-related infant to raise.

At the other end of the spectrum, it is in the name of autonomy that many have argued for patients' rights to choose their own death in the face of suffering, and to have the help of sympathetic physicians in dying when they find the burdens of their existence too great. I will consider the merits and the problems of such arguments from a Christian standpoint in some detail in Chapter 3, where I discuss how the duties expressed in the principles of bioethics might be understood and honored in difficult or disputed cases. But claims like these also provide an appropriate background for the next section where I look at the theological reasons Christians have for affirming some versions of a duty to respect patient autonomy, and for rejecting or reinterpreting others.

Autonomy: Theological Foundations and Critique

St. Augustine, Bishop of Hippo in the fourth century, was one of the first theologians to deal directly and explicitly with the nature of the person which is implied by Christian faith. Augustine develops his picture of human nature in terms of the trinitarian being of God in whose image we are made. He begins by characterizing the Persons of the Trinity according to their role in the divine economy, and explaining how human beings reflect the nature of each.

God the Father is the ultimately Real, the self-subsistent One who is the source of all that is and of being itself. Human beings, like all things that exist, do so by participating in this divine being in a reduced and contingent fashion. In this sense, everything in creation reflects some tiny portion of God's glory simply by being existent rather than non-existent. Living beings are yet more like God, in that they share not only existence but life, and thus reveal more of the nature of God who is Life itself. So, we are like God first in being, and in being alive.

Christ the Son is the Logos, usually translated as the Word of God, but meaning also the Wisdom or the Knowledge or the Reason of God. Human beings not only exist and are alive, but they know that they live. They are unique in being self-aware and self-reflective, capable of thinking about themselves and other beings in the world, and even of being consciously aware of their Creator. In this capacity to know, to reflect on reality and to abstract from it and reason about it, they image Christ who is the Knowledge of God made flesh in the world. So we are like God not only in being and being alive, but in knowing ourselves as alive and in being able to reason about the meaning of our existence.

Finally, from God the source of all being and Christ the Word and Wisdom of God proceeds the Holy Spirit, whom Augustine characterizes as the Love proceeding from the eternal union of Father and Son. Human beings not only exist and live and know their own existence, they love and rejoice in their own being. They are capable of loving the rest of God's creation, and of knowing and loving God their Creator, Redeemer, and Sustainer as God is revealed to them. "Loving" in Augustine's language means not only rejoicing in, but also desiring and pursuing. The attraction to what we love is for Augustine the spring of all human action; it is our loves which drive our choosing. So, in our capacity not merely to exist but to know reflectively that we exist, to love and choose what we pursue and to know that we are doing so, we reflect the three Persons of the Trinity. It is how we bear the image of God.

Not all accounts of what it means to be in God's image have the elegance of Augustine's discussion, but his stress on the confluence of reason and love in human choice has been enormously powerful in Christian thought. For Christians, the obligation to respect all persons is based on the obligation to recognize and honor the image of God that each of them is. The notion that we are like God in our capacity for reflective and responsible choice makes the guarding of human freedom and responsibility a matter of most serious theological import.

In fact, the whole biblical drama sketched in the previous chapter arises because even the fulfillment of our intended relation with God is bounded by our freedom, which even God will not violate; the loving union to which God calls us cannot be coerced. While the relationship with God is understood in Scripture as normative, indeed as the whole sum and purpose of human existence, it has nonetheless a kind of privacy and privilege. (This is the reason for Paul's scrupulous care to protect conscience even when it is in error.) So Christians have distinctive and compelling reasons for taking the claims of autonomy, linked closely with the liberty and integrity of conscience, with great seriousness.

On the other hand, they also have distinctive and compelling reasons to be suspicious of the claims of human autonomy, or at least of many accounts of them. Christians cannot affirm understandings of autonomy which develop the concept of human freedom in isolation from the claims of relation with and responsibility toward other human beings. The picture of the self-possessed individual deciding his or her own fate in splendid isolation is one wholly alien to the Christian understanding of moral existence.

They must also resist those versions of autonomy which violate another fundamental Christian conviction: God's sovereignty over human life. For as we have seen in even our brief look at the biblical tradition which forms us, humans do not exist alone, or for themselves simply. They exist together and for one another as well—and ultimately they exist for God, for the sake of that friendship with God into which human beings are called. As we have already noted, from this standpoint, human life is not a possession but a gift and a trust. Your body is your own in the sense that you are most intimately and inseparably connected with it, and it is the locus and condition of your experience—but it is not a thing over which you can have property rights. You did not buy it, you cannot replace it, you cannot even (in the words of a famous man) add an inch to its stature. Those who receive Jesus Christ as Savior and Lord must confess with Paul, "You are not your own, you were bought with a price" (1 Cor. 6:19-20), and recognize that they are wholly, body and spirit, claimed by the one who redeems them. This is the framework that makes sense of Paul's advice, "Present your bodies as a living sacrifice, which is your reasonable worship . . ." (Rom. 12:1).

So does all this mean that someone else ought to determine what happens to a patient in the hospital, what treatment is given and what goals are pursued? It definitely does not. But the decisions of patients and their families are to be made in a moral context formed by the story of creation, call and redemption. They are to be made in the recognition that each of us is the responsible and accountable steward of the gift of life—and the steward is not the owner. We have obligations to ourselves as God's called and beloved, to other people as our companions on the way, and to God as Savior and Lord for what we do or do not do to care for and sustain our lives.

This is the context in which some of the traditional norms in medical ethics were shaped, and in which they make sense. It is the rationale, for example, for the distinction between "ordinary" treatment (which is morally obligatory) and "extraordinary" treatment (which is optional). In its original (Roman Catholic) formulation, the obligation is thought of as owed not solely to the patient, but also *by* the patient to God as Author and "owner" of life. This is also the background to the traditional Christian opposition to suicide. Both rest upon the conviction that our lives do not belong to us in so sweeping a sense as to be at our disposal. When this claim is coupled with the understanding that suffering is an evil but not the ultimate evil, not something we may do anything whatever in order to prevent, it also provides the basis for the long-standing belief that we ought not kill a patient to relieve or prevent suffering. There are, in short, theological constraints on what autonomy may mean and upon what it may authorize. They arise from the fact that ours is a real but also a *created* freedom. It is sustained and not opposed by God—but it is a liberty bounded by the limits inherent in being creatures, who are neither the source nor the end of their own existence.

Non-Maleficence: Definition and Application

The principle of non-maleficence simply expresses the obligation not to cause harm. It is often spoken of in medical contexts as founded upon the Hippocratic maxim *primum non nocere* ("first, do no harm").[2] In bioethics, this principle serves as a barrier against using the enormous power conferred by medical knowledge and technique in ways that injure rather than benefit patients. Thus, the oaths taken by nurses and physicians include promises not to perform harmful or unnecessary procedures, and they promise due care and diligence to protect patients from error, neglect and abuse. The kinds of harm in view in medicine include pain, disability, disfigurement, bodily damage, and death. For health care providers to risk these outcomes (for example, by using an untested medication) also counts as a harm, in the same way that endangering a minor is a crime even if the child is not actually hurt.

Of course, the duty not to inflict these harms is not and cannot be absolute. If it were, most medical procedures would be ruled out, since even a vaccination causes some pain and entails some risk. Other procedures, such as the amputation of a limb, create a certain and permanent condition of serious disability. Instead, the obligation is understood to rule out actions whose total effect is harmful, those in which the harm suffered is not offset by avoiding a greater harm or providing a greater benefit. The obligation of care givers is to perform no treatment which *on balance* does harm to the patient, where the harms prevented or the goods secured do not outweigh the risks and burdens of the treatment.

In making judgments about harms and benefits, the patient is considered as a whole organism rather than as a set of organs and systems. Called "the principle of totality," this is the understanding that justifies even a radical treatment such as amputation if it is necessary to preserve the health of the whole body; the welfare of the part is subordinated to the welfare of the whole. The removal of a limb is changed from an act of mutilation to a life-saving surgical procedure by its contribution to the well-being of the patient threatened by gangrene.

The duty not to inflict harm has usually been taken as more primary and more stringent than duties to prevent or remedy harm, or duties to provide positive benefits. This is true in general as well as in medical contexts. For instance, everyone recognizes an obligation not to push someone in front of a moving car. On the other hand, efforts to rescue someone about to be hit or to care for an accident victim are thought of as weaker duties, or even not as duties at all. They may fall into the category called "supererogatory," things it would be good to do but that it is not wrong to omit. Thus we often regard people who try to rescue others whose plight they did not cause as heroes. People who do nothing in such circumstances are not admired, but they aren't blamed unless their role or job gives them a special obligation to help (like a parent or a police officer). Everyone, however, is strictly required not to cause harm to others whether by actions or by neglect.

The observation that our duties not to cause harm are stronger than our duties to help explains why the principle of non-maleficence in medicine is generally considered to take precedence over the care givers' aim to help the sick. In fact, the necessity of avoiding harm frequently acts as a limit on means that may be used to benefit the sick. For example, not even the desire to find a cure for a terrible disease can justify medical research methods which injure human subjects or place them at great risk. Non-maleficence also places limits on how and from whom life-saving organ donations can be asked for or accepted. Even though a particular organ may be urgently needed to save a patient's life, a physician may not do anything to hasten the death of the potential organ donor, even if that person is already dying. The need to protect the vulnerable from harm also makes physicians very reluctant to accept donations of paired organs, like kidneys, from minors or from those who are otherwise not competent to consent, even when close relationship makes these donors medically the best candidates.

This relative priority of non-maleficence also shapes public policy in areas like the testing and approval of new medications and devices. Even though the speedy approval of a new drug may benefit thousands of patients suffering from the condition it treats, the primary mission of the Food and Drug Administration and similar agencies around the world is to prevent harm caused by drugs which have not been fully tested. Recently, the struggle to find effective treatments for AIDS has generated some pressure to speed up the drug approval process. Nevertheless, those instances where the mission to prevent harm has failed (like the infamous Thalidomide disaster of the early 1960s, in which an anti-nausea drug produced devastating birth defects) have proven more powerful in the public imagination than the frustrations caused by delay. The specter of physician-caused injury is worse than medical impotence.

The stringent duty not to injure by medical means is a central aspect of the role of health care providers in our society. It decisively shapes public expectations of them, but even more significantly it is central in their own self-understanding of what it means to be a good nurse or doctor. The commitment not to harm is the basis of the refusal of most physicians to participate in judicial executions. It is also the foundation of the widespread (although not universal) resistance of doctors to using active measures to cause death as in euthanasia or physician-assisted suicide.

We all have a great stake in preserving this crucial virtue of the profession, for in recent times we have seen the horrors that result when these internalized barriers are wholly subverted or overcome, as they were in Germany during the Nazi era. Doctors directed and participated in the medical execution of the handicapped and the mentally ill, and in brutal and fatal experiments using concentration camp inmates to test how the body responds to trauma. The crimes of murder and torture of the innocent were exacerbated by the perversion of medical authority, and by the betrayal of the trust lodged in those to whom we turn for care.

But the fact that few medical treatments cause no harm whatever, and few are wholly without risk, forces upon care givers the task of weighing the burdens and risks of procedures against the potential benefits they offer. Part of the difficulty of doing so lies in the fact (already noted) that the likelihood of benefit or harm in individual cases is a matter of clinical judgment. They can be "objectively" weighed only after the fact and over a large number of trials, and it is not easy to know what to do with statistical information about a treatment's likely results. But more difficult still is reaching clarity about what count as benefits and harms, and how they are to be weighed against one another.

This is why the principle of non-maleficence has been used to argue both *for* and *against* various kinds of treatment, such as artificial feeding of comatose patients, or aggressive intervention for terminally ill or severely handicapped newborns. In cases like these, where the long-term survival prospects for the patients are poor to non-existent, the bodily invasion and discomfort that go with "doing everything we can"—which may include respirators, catheters, feeding tubes, central IV lines, massive doses of drugs or radiation, and multiple resuscitation efforts, among other things—may seem only to prolong the dying process. They may be seen to inflict a worse dying, or a survival so minimal and fraught with such struggle that its continuation is an injury rather than a benefit.

However, it is also possible to see withholding such things as drugs or surgery for the desperately ill, or artificial food and water for the permanently unconscious, as a failure to provide life-sustaining care. Particularly when the immediate cause of death is a curable condition, or is starvation and/or dehydration following the ending of artificial food and water, it is easy to charge care givers with doing harm. The fact that the death comes as the result of an omission rather than an act is little help, since medical neglect is also counted a harm.

The only way finally to resolve such disagreements is by placing the discussion of what counts as a harm or a benefit into a wider context: one where it is possible to talk about why life is important, why we should try to sustain it, and when it might be appropriate to relinquish our struggle for it. For Christians, that means returning to the ways of thinking and speaking which belong to our own tradition, to the story we tell and the ways of living that witness to it.

Non-Maleficence: Theological Foundations and Critique

The Christian theological foundations of a general and universal duty not to harm are straightforward and compelling. To lay them out will largely recap what I have already said in the opening chapter on the character of Christian ethics.

Every person we encounter is, like us, created by God for particular friendship with God, and has the same source and destiny as we have. Within the community, everyone is met as one "for whom Christ died" (1 Cor. 8:11) and as Christ himself meeting us in "the least of these [his] followers" (Matt. 25:40). The statement, "whatever you did to the least of these you did to me" effectively rules out the possibility that we might deliberately or carelessly harm the sister or brother in any context, much less the medical one in which we have taken on responsibility for a person who is vulnerable because of illness.

Outside the community, we encounter persons as belonging to the universal category of the neighbor, a group which expressly includes the outcast and the enemy. They are to be the objects of our concern, are to be honored (1 Pet. 2:17), and in particular are not to be harmed or insulted even when they are themselves guilty of unprovoked attack upon us (Matt. 5:39; 1 Pet. 3:9). If even the assault of enemies is not to call forth an answering attack, then clearly the innocent are not to be harmed, either by action or by neglect.

In the medical context, the general obligation not to harm is greatly strengthened by the special duties of the care giver. For we do not enter health care facilities merely as private individuals relating to other private individuals: we enter as patients, who give nurses and doctors special and intimate access to our bodies and our confidences; or we enter as care givers, who are pledged to use the power conferred by our training and our position only to help and never to harm those entrusted to us. Thus, we enter as participants in a kind of covenant, with obligations to keep faith with each other in the shared task of stewardship over the gift of life. Within this privileged relationship, the care giver is pledged not only to avoid deliberate harm, but to exercise professional skill, care and diligence to see that harm and risk are avoided or minimized. As in all relationships of covenant and promise, the model for this relationship is God's relationship with God's people, in which God resolutely keeps faith despite the inconstancy and rebellion of humankind.

The depth and the weight of the responsibilities that flow from the covenant between the sick and those caring for them are not fully captured in the flat and commercial language of the contract. On that model, the obligations of parties cease and the relationship is dissolved upon the failure of either side to perform as agreed. When medical care is viewed in this way, it is simply a service rendered for a fee, and the inability to pay is a sufficient ground for denying care. The moral poverty of such a view is recognized even in law, where a physician is obliged to give care in an emergency to anyone needing it; even private hospitals must stabilize a critically ill patient before transfer to a public facility.[3]

But if Christian convictions provide a foundation for a strong obligation not to harm, still Christian moral thought does not always share common medical ethical assessments of what count as harms, or how they are to be compared to one another. In general, the notion of goods and harms under which bioethics usually operates is too narrow and too materialist (in the philosophical sense of assuming that all reality consists of matter) from a Christian standpoint. It tends to take account of physical harms, of psychological harms at the outside, and to disregard the category of moral and spiritual harms altogether. Above all, it tends to focus upon the avoidance of death, seen as the ultimate harm. For example, we have already alluded to the fashion in which medical ethics tolerates the behavior of Jehovah's Witnesses who refuse blood transfusions. Their refusal is treated purely as an exercise of autonomy, as part of the liberty of adults to make even bad choices without coercion. This does not really deal with the Witness's contention that by the use of blood, the benefit of temporal life is being bought at too high a price (which is, in their view, eternal damnation).

While most Christians reject the idiosyncratic exegesis of Leviticus on which the prohibition of transfusions is based,[4] the notion that some prices even for life itself may be too high is one with which they must have some sympathy. After all, the church owes its existence to people who faced death rather than commit acts of idolatry: who risked imprisonment in disease-infested jails rather than keep silent about their faith; who accepted burning rather than "soil their souls" with false recantations. And Christians follow One who promises, "the one who loses his life for my sake will gain it" (Mark 8:35).

The inclusion of intangible, spiritual gains and losses within the horizon of benefits and harms considered in medicine does more than provide an alternative foundation for the duty to respect claims of conscience. The conviction that not death but final separation from God is the evil to be avoided at all costs requires making treatment decisions in light of the overriding necessity of keeping faith with God and each other. This may take the form of declining life-extending treatment because of the unjust burdens it places on others, or conversely of accepting burdensome treatment for the sake of obligations to others it allows one to fulfill. It may mean refusing options such as active euthanasia or suicide which violate Christian notions of God's sovereignty over life, or refusing treatment methods that are thought to infringe on our duties to each other, such as the acceptance of organ donations from donors who are put at risk. It also makes sense of decisions which risk even fatal harm for the sake of our ties to others, like that of the mother mentioned in the previous chapter who declined chemotherapy in order safely to deliver her child.

A second critique or qualification of how the principle of non-maleficence is employed is related to the understanding of suffering sketched in the previous chapter. I have already tried to show why Christians, who worship a God who overcomes sin and redeems the world through the willing and innocent suffering of Christ, cannot evaluate physical suffering (or for that matter, any suffering) as the worst possible evil, the ultimate enemy. They must therefore be critical of arguments which take our duty to prevent harm to mean that it would be better actively to end the lives of the chronically sick or impaired, whether terminal or not, in order to relieve their suffering or that of their families. Such arguments assume that suffering is not only a historical evil, but unredeemable, unable to be transformed, and hence to be avoided at any cost. By contrast, those formed by the story of Jesus Christ and his followers share a picture of human life as discipleship which can and *must be able to* take up, endure, and make sense (and even good) out of the evil of suffering. It is a capacity which they must not abandon or denigrate. By the story they tell and the life they embrace, Christians are committed to the view that it is not irrational to choose a course which will entail suffering or even death as the price of integrity, or of love.

Beneficence: Definition and Application

The principle of beneficence expresses a general duty to help other persons. In bioethics, it expresses the obligation of medical practitioners to do positive good to their patients. In the medical context, this includes preventing death or disability, relieving suffering, effecting cure or amelioration where possible, and furthering the health-related interests and aims of the patient. There is no fixed and sharp distinction between the duty to avoid harm and the duty to provide benefit, as the inclusion of "preventing death" in the list suggests. However, beneficence generally refers to positive efforts undertaken to sustain or improve a patient's health, whereas nonmaleficence concerns harms we are to refrain from inflicting.

If avoiding harm is the crucial negative duty of medical practice, the obligation to help the sick and the suffering is its heart, and the whole *raison d'etre* of medicine as an art. Serving the patient's good is the rationale of all medical treatment, and the central "role-specific" obligation of care givers to their patients. It is this service to the welfare of patients which justifies the enormous prestige and power conferred upon doctors in particular in our society. Physicians and nurses have unparalleled access to other people, both to their physical bodies and to their fears, their vulnerabilities, and their secrets. Their judgment is often deferred to in non-medical as well as medical matters, and in them people repose their trust, confidence and hope. All of this makes the assumption of the role of care giver a matter of great moral seriousness, and gives the special obligations of beneficence which belong to that role tremendous weight. Nevertheless, as indicated in the discussions of autonomy and of non-maleficence above, the duty to benefit patients cannot be absolute, and it is not always overriding. It may be overcome by obligations to respect patients' decisions, as when clearly helpful or even life-saving treatments are steadfastly refused; and it may be limited by the obligation not to cause harm, whether to the patient or to some other person.

The obligations of medical practitioners to help are limited also by their own reasonable needs and interests. No one expects nurses and doctors to work without rest, without compensation, or in circumstances that place them at high risk of grave harm (although the devotion of physicians who have cared for the destitute, or the heroic risks taken by doctors and nurses in times of plague, have been part of the ethos and ideals of medicine for centuries and remain part of the mystique of medical practice). Despite these recognized limits, to help patients is the whole reason that care givers practice their profession, and it is frustrating and painful for them as well as for their patients when they are forced by circumstances or by the intrinsic limits of medical capacity to say, "There is nothing more we can do." These frustrations are apparent in two of the classic problems in bioethics, both of which arise as the duty to benefit conflicts with other obligations. These are the problems of paternalism in medicine, and of the ethics of medical research.

Paternalism is the name given to actions in which a care giver overrides a patient's autonomy, either by deception or by coercion, for the sake of benefiting the patient. One such case was mentioned earlier in the discussion of the voluntariness of patient consent for treatment.[5] Other examples are when patients are lied to about their condition or prognosis (often at the family's urging) because their doctors think the truth will be too painful, or will endanger a patient who is fragile or unstable. However, this deception effectively prevents the patient from participating in a meaningful way in decisions about treatment, and may also keep patients and their families from making preparations for death or other foreseeable events.

Other instances of paternalism occur when a patient's wishes, whether for treatment or against it, are overridden because they will cause preventable harm to the patient or to someone else; all instances of involuntary commitment to psychiatric hospitals take this form. Everyone acknowledges that some cases (children, the delusional, the severely retarded, et al.) may require someone else to act in the patient's best interest without consent. The controversy is over when this kind of protective intervention is warranted, and how we are to decide.

Cases like psychiatric commitment are conceptually quite clear. Forced hospitalization is supposed to be limited to those who are a danger to themselves or to others, and whose capacity to make a reasonable decision about their own care is reduced by mental disturbance or disease. In practical reality, making and defending judgments of this kind is notoriously difficult and subjective.[6] Not only are psychiatry and psychology very poor predictors of human behavior, but judgments about mental health or illness are infiltrated by social and cultural factors and evaluations. A poor, homeless person, or someone who does not speak English well, is more likely to be judged incompetent or dangerous than an educated and affluent person. Women are more likely to be assessed as incompetent than men, even though there is a statistically higher incidence of mental illness in men than in women. Thus, even though it is easy to justify intervening to protect the welfare of those who are unable to protect themselves, it is much more difficult to figure out who belongs in that category.

The other kind of case, in which a generally competent patient is deceived or coerced for "her [or his] own good," is more difficult to defend even in theory. Of course news about a debilitating or terminal illness will be shocking, painful, or frightening. It would hardly be normal to be unaffected by such information. But the fact remains that the foreseen events will occur, and the patient will be forced to deal with them whether they are named or not. Withholding information about their condition from the sick over any long period can only add to patients' sense of betrayal and isolation, and deprive them of the chance to make their struggles their own. For these reasons, even the duty to benefit the patient is not usually thought to excuse paternalistic deceptions in cases of this kind. Only the most extreme danger to a patient in crisis can justify keeping vital information about condition or prognosis from a competent patient, and then only until the crisis is resolved.

Besides forming the basis of interventions to protect the welfare of incompetent patients, the duty to do good to patients, present and future, provides the justification for medical research involving human subjects. Such research falls into two categories. *Therapeutic research* involves the use of experimental or unproven therapies or techniques in the treatment of patients when there is at least reasonable hope that the patient/subject will benefit. *Non-therapeutic research* involves either patients or healthy volunteers in research to advance medical or scientific knowledge. Here the benefits will be to society in general, or to future patients for whom treatments might be developed.

Like medical treatment, participation in research requires informed consent, with all the features laid out above. In non-therapeutic research in particular, where the patient is not even the intended beneficiary, the requirements for ensuring that patient/subjects are genuinely free and informed are very stringent. For example, children, prisoners, military recruits, and even medical students are morally excluded from all but the most risk-free research on the grounds that their freedom to refuse is limited or compromised.

Furthermore, to gain the approval of review boards which control access to funding, research proposals must demonstrate that the expected benefits for subjects or future patients outweigh the possible risks or harms. Even with full consent, there are limits on what degree of pain, risk or inconvenience may be imposed on human subjects. No one may authorize non-therapeutic experiments which place subjects at high risk of death or injury, or which cause severe pain, no matter how useful the information gained might be. Here, as in medicine generally, the duty not to cause harm takes precedence over the obligation to provide benefit.

Even with these constraints, conflicts sometimes arise between the goals of medical research and the best interests of patient/subjects. For example, when two different drugs are being compared for their effectiveness in treating an illness, researchers may become convinced that a new drug is substantially more effective than the standard treatment to which it is being compared. However, they may not have sufficient data to publish their findings, and thus to change the standard therapy for future patients. The question arises, Should the study be terminated early so that all subjects may receive the more effective drug, or not? The conflict is between the duty to help present patients who are research subjects, and the duty to help other and future sufferers from the same disease by advancing the state of therapy. Most theorists resolve such conflicts in favor of the interests of research subjects on the ground that the physician conducting trials has weightier obligations to existing patients. They advocate stopping clinical trials early if a researcher is convinced that one therapy offers substantially more benefit than the alternative.

Beneficence: Theological Foundations and Critique

Beneficence is the easiest of all principles to ground in Christian faith, in that the obligation to help the sick is simply a special case of the universal obligation to love the neighbor. We have seen in Chapter 1 how broad and central this duty is, and how concrete and far-reaching in its implications. Neighbors explicitly include strangers and enemies (e.g., Matt. 5:43; Luke 6:27; 1 Pet. 2:23). And the love which is commanded is not sentimental, but active and practical: "If your enemy is hungry, feed him; if he is thirsty, give him drink" (Rom. 12:20, RSV).

By contrast, most contemporary moral philosophers have been reluctant to treat the giving of help to others to whom we have neither special relations nor promises as a strong obligation. They generally treat beneficence as either a weak duty, easily defeated by conflicting interests, or as supererogatory, praiseworthy but not mandatory. The reason is that a strenuous duty to help others seems to place demands on our lives and our resources which are not compatible with the understanding of personal liberty and autonomy which prevails in our culture. We are encouraged to think of our lives as our own, and of any obligation that calls for a substantial change in our goals and plans for ourselves as intrusive. Christians, however, have quite a different starting point, one which places them in permanent "indebtedness" to God. They are not "self-possessed" and cannot think of themselves as "self-made," but rather as abundantly gifted and graced by God to whom they give themselves in response. Thus, active love of the neighbor is not simply a choice or an option for Christians, but the central obligation which orders all others.

So the effect of Christian convictions is to strengthen and broaden the obligation of beneficence. Moreover, we have seen how the New Testament's accounts of love and of faithfulness include the possibility of substantial risk and self-sacrifice for the sake of fulfilling the positive demands of love. The more vigorous account of the moral duty of beneficence which results has direct implications for medical ethics, both at the level of clinical practice and at the wider level of public policy and the understanding of social obligations in medicine.

Christian ethicists generally argue on the basis of beneficence and justice for a duty to provide a decent minimum of medical treatment to all those in need, apart from ability to pay. They also tend to support changes in our current system of health care delivery to fulfill this obligation. The contrasting position taken by the American Medical Association (AMA), which opposed most health care reform proposals in the recent public debate, is instructive. While recognizing that physicians have a duty to do good to their patients, the AMA has insisted that doctors alone should determine who those patients will be. It has asserted principles[7] which include treating doctors as entrepreneurs, private contractors who may treat whomever they will for as long as they choose and no longer.

The position of the AMA is grounded on the autonomy of physicians, and on the investment of time, money, and effort they have made in their medical educations. While such a position may be defensible within the individualist moral framework of our society, it amounts to treating the skills of health care givers as personal possessions which they may contract to exchange with a willing purchaser on whatever terms they choose. On this view, medicine is a commodity like any other. This is not finally compatible with the traditional understanding of medicine as a moral art and a public trust. It is also markedly at odds with Christian understandings of moral life, in which all of one's gifts and abilities are understood as bestowed by God for the sake of the welfare of the community.

In such a climate, it is not surprising that there has arisen some controversy about whether doctors and nurses have a duty to treat AIDS patients or those with other dangerous infectious diseases. This is the case even though the actual risk for practitioners of contracting AIDS in the delivery of health care is extremely small: much smaller than the risks encountered by all physicians before the advent of antibiotics, or even before the recent development of a vaccine for hepatitis B.[8] This is a place where the essential place of the virtue of courage in Christian moral life, and the importance of the confidence in God which sustains it, become evident. It may be that the moral traditions of medicine, built on a religious foundation by Hippocrates so many centuries ago, require some such foundation for their support.

Justice: Definition and Application

At its most general, the principle of justice concerns the fair sharing of the benefits and burdens of a society among its members. In medicine, this principle applies both to the procedures by which medical care is provided for individuals (procedural justice), and to how the resources of medicine are distributed between individual patients and groups of patients (distributive justice). In the first (procedural) category belong issues about how we decide who receives care, how long they must wait for it, and what quality of care they have access to. An egregious and well-known case of injustice at this level is the treatment of the famous gospel and blues singer Bessie Smith, who was injured along with her manager in a car accident in Alabama in 1934. The manager, who was a white man, was treated promptly at the nearest hospital, and recovered from his injuries. Ms. Smith was denied care because the hospital did not treat black people, and bled to death on the long ride to the nearest facility that would admit "Negroes."

Issues of justice in the second, or distributive, category fall into two groups. Problems of *microallocation* concern who receives a scarce medical resource when there is not enough for everyone who needs it. Common examples include transplantable organs, supplies of a rare blood type, and beds in an Intensive Care Unit when there are not enough in a given area. Decisions about who should receive such resources are made on a mixture of different grounds. First there are medical criteria like the urgency of the patient's need and the likelihood of long-term benefit, which reflect the concern that life-saving care not be wasted. When the medical criteria have been satisfied, there are moral criteria like maintaining commitments to existing patients, and recognizing basic human equality by procedures like a lottery, or a strict first-come-first-served policy.

Problems of *macroallocation* in medicine have to do with how the funds and time available for medical research and treatment are divided up among different health care needs, technologies, and lines of inquiry. Should a city hospital invest in the expensive technology that may allow it to save the lives of very premature newborns, or in neighborhood outreach programs which offer prenatal care for poor mothers? Should tax dollars support the development of an artificial heart to extend the lives of heart disease patients for whom other means are not available, or should they be devoted to research aimed at improving treatment for crippling arthritis? It is always tempting to say that we should do all of these things, but the fact is that resources are limited and needs will always outstrip them. Deciding what portion of a society's funds, energy and talent should go to health care, rather than to education or environmental protection or some other worthy goal, is also a problem of macroallocation.

Obviously, decisions made on the larger scale about what resources to place in medicine and where have an impact on what decisions one is forced to make on the smaller scale. When mechanical kidney dialysis first became available, there were not enough of the expensive machines to support all of the people who would die without them. This created a need to decide who would have access to these life-saving machines. The committees appointed to allocate dialysis time argued over the weight of factors like age, parental responsibilities, moral merit and even expected earning power in deciding who should be kept alive. The moral quandaries and controversies which arose as committees pondered the relative merits, needs, and contributions of candidates for dialysis did much to force the development of bioethics as a discipline. It also caused such public outcry that in 1973 Congress established the End Stage Renal Disease program of Medicare to provide federal funding for dialysis to all who need it to survive.

This has avoided the necessity of "God committees" (as they were popularly dubbed) to determine which dialysis patients would be kept alive. On the other hand, it has also created an enormous drain on resources, with a multi-billion-dollar price tag over twenty-plus years. Moreover, it has not eliminated the necessity of making similar decisions for other kinds of treatment by less obvious means such as deciding what Medicaid treatments to pay for and for whom, or what treatments private insurers may exclude as "experimental" and refuse to cover. Despite all the complexities and unresolved questions that have been mentioned in the discussion of earlier principles, questions about justice in health care remain the most intractable. This is partly due to the competing understandings of justice or fairness which operate in our society.

The history of the debate over who should receive dialysis illustrates all the various and quite distinct things we may mean when we speak of someone being "entitled to" something, or when we claim that some benefit has been fairly or unfairly received. It turns out that there are many grounds on which to parcel out different kinds of benefits, and which one is appropriate depends on what is being distributed. We expect prizes for races to be handed out based on performance: whoever finishes first without breaking the rules should win. Students are often outraged if grades do not seem uniformly based on performance, although they may also expect some consideration to be given to effort.

Other kinds of benefits are strictly universal, distributed in equal shares; every citizen is entitled to exactly one vote in elections, everyone has an equal right to protection by the law, etc. By contrast, we want awards for outstanding community service to be given on the basis of contributions to society, and things like Nobel prizes on the basis of merit and achievement. Other things we accept ought to be distributed based on need. Subsidies for food and rent, compensation for injuries or disability, special educational services: all these ought to go to all those who need them, and only to them. Finally, most Americans think some things should be distributed according to the ability to pay for them. We think this way about large houses, expensive cars, vacation trips and other things that fall into the category of luxuries. The question we face is, On what basis do we decide who should get access to what share of medical care?

In the United States, a patchwork of different mechanisms and programs provide access to health care, operating under a variety of principles of distribution. Publicly supported health care in the form of state- or federally-funded programs is available to the very poor, to the disabled, and to persons aged sixty-five and over. The first two categories are distributed according to need, the third according to a kind of entitlement established by law for persons of retirement age, whether they are in financial need or not. (Of course, all of these forms of guaranteed access to health care for the poor and elderly are under reconsideration by Congress as this is being written.)

Most Americans' access to health care depends on private group health insurance subsidized by employers, which ties health care access to employment status and indirectly to income. This may be seen as distribution according to social contribution if (and only if) employment compensation is thought to be distributed fairly according to merit and effort. Veterans of American military service with financial need are entitled to free medical care at special facilities across the nation, a clearer example of distribution according to social contribution. Other individuals, such as the self-employed or those whose jobs provide no benefits, must purchase expensive individual or family health insurance, or do without such insurance and often without primary health care unless medical debt forces them below the poverty line. These individuals' access to health care is tied directly to income. Finally, other individuals can afford to pay privately for whatever health care they need; like the preceding group, these people's access depends directly on their ability to pay for health care.

There are also people in our society who fall into none of these categories, who have no reliable access to any kind of health care. These include undocumented immigrants, homeless people (who have no fixed address and thus are ineligible for state-based Medicaid), and people with problems including substance addiction which are not recognized as disabilities. What health care they do receive is provided by overburdened hospital emergency rooms, or by a variety of private service organizations, many of them church-supported. Often that care is both more costly and less effective than prompt primary care would have been; sometimes, it comes altogether too late. These people suffer and die of treatable or preventable illnesses at a much higher rate than those with stable access to care.

The recent public debate about reforming the health care financing system in the United States uncovered both areas of broad consensus and areas of deep disagreement about what a just system of health care allocation would look like. There are some broadly shared understandings which form the basis for arguing that everyone should have access to whatever level of basic medical care a society can support for all its members. The first of these concerns the character of health itself as a primary and fundamental good, one which makes possible the reception of all other goods and benefits. Since without some degree of physical health no one can either contribute to society or enjoy its benefits, support for it is basic for both individual and social well-being.

The second basis for a goal of universal access is the idea that health and disease are largely random features of life, distributed by accident or natural lottery and not according to desert.[9] Since children with genetic defects or patients with diabetes do not somehow deserve their lot, efforts to cure or reduce the bad effects of these conditions are appropriate efforts to share the burdens of human society.

The final argument for universal access based in justice is the recognition that the techniques, the skills and the resources of medical care and research are socially supported. They are furthered by the participation of all citizens through taxes, and through public subsidies of research and of capital improvements in health care facilities. Both care and research also receive significant support from donations and from voluntary participation in research by millions. All members of the society contribute to some degree, and therefore all have some claim to benefit.

Although there is a broad acceptance of the idea that access to "basic care" or "a decent minimum" of health care should be universal, there is little agreement about what that minimum should include, and even less about what trade-offs should be made in order to provide universal access. To put it another way, there is scant willingness on the part of the majority of Americans to compromise any of the quality, convenience or personal discretion which they now have in their medical care, even for the sake of caring for those now excluded. This may be seen simply as narrow self-interest, a reflection of our individualistic moral culture. It may also be seen as the effect of competing ideas of justice; those who link just distribution to moral merit and social contribution are more prepared to see the poor, illegal residents, and those who are addicted to drugs as justly excluded from the health care system.

Justice: Theological Foundations and Critique

Christian sources for the duty of justice are woven throughout the tradition. Most fundamental is the doctrine of creation, which grounds the basic equality and dignity of all human beings in their divine origin. As bearers of God's image and subjects of God's care, all persons have claims against attack, claims to equitable treatment, and claims not to be unfairly excluded from the resources that all need for well-being. Given the thoroughly social picture of human life found in the Bible, it is not surprising that all three kinds of justice-based claims are elaborated and specified in the texts of the Old and New Testaments.

The Books of the Law lay out penalties for criminal violations.

They specify punishments for premeditated murder, crimes of impulse and involuntary or accidental manslaughter as well as various kinds of theft, fraud, and assault. They also concern themselves with how transactions are to be managed and claims of injury settled, laying the foundations of tort law in the provisions of Leviticus. In addition, a great deal of attention is given to the fair treatment of laborers, and to the protections which are to be provided for the poor and to vulnerable groups like widows and orphans. These include not only laws concerning the fair recognition of their rights in marketplace and courtroom, but provisions which secure a portion of the harvest for their use.

There are also laws which require the forgiveness of debts after seven years, and land which has been mortgaged is to be returned to the original owners every fifty years. These are laws designed to prevent absolute destitution for the poor, and also to prevent the development of entrenched economic classes based on land ownership in an agrarian society. When the violations of covenant provisions against poverty bring about a permanent underclass (the words of Deut. 15:11 about the poor being always there are a reproach to Israel, not an excuse; cf. Deut. 15:4), then the poor and vulnerable are taken to be special subjects of God's care.

There are two aspects of the Old Testament understanding of justice which are especially important to an understanding of justice in medical care, and both are underlined in the writings of the prophets and echoed in the New Testament. The first is that justice includes *both* fair procedures *and* social institutions that protect the weakest members of society. The second is that justice is consistently treated as a matter of faith; it is the hallmark of a society ordered by trust in the God who is universal in love and impartial in judgment. When the prophets denounce the evils that will bring down God's judgment on Israel, prominent in their indictment is the perversion of instruments of justice, and the neglect of those in need.

No less scathing is the attack in James 5:1-6, which denounces not only judicial corruption but also the indifference of the rich who feast while others go hungry. Throughout the prophetic writings, God's vindication of the oppressed is one of the hallmarks of the messianic era. Thus, Jesus answers the question of John's disciples about his identity by pointing out "the poor have good news preached to them" (Luke 7:22). Overall, the Bible makes it clear that equity in treatment, procedural equality and just distribution of goods are all aspects of the reign of God over the world, and obligatory for God's people.

There is, therefore, considerable tension between some philosophical accounts of justice, and biblical and Christian versions. Rooted in the classical understanding of justice as securing "to each one his due," philosophical theories have often been rigorous only at the level of formal justice: similar treatment for similar cases. For example, Aristotle, who could dispassionately consider whether or not women and slaves had rational souls, had no trouble with the idea that what was "due" to them was subordination and the direction of their betters. Philosophers have frequently insisted that each should receive what each deserves, without clearly defining how we know what is deserved by each. We have already seen how a number of distinct notions of justice or fairness operate within our own society in various contexts. Effort, market mechanisms, social contribution, moral merit, and age have all been proposed as bases on which to decide not only who receives honors or luxuries, but who receives necessities, including medical care.

The biblical picture of justice, with its emphasis not only on procedural justice but also on substantive notions of just distribution according to need, is not neutral about these competing theories. "First-come-first-served" approaches, or lottery-based systems which use randomness to represent equal claims, are defensible. So is the use of standards involving a patient's medical fitness as a candidate for a particular treatment, and the probability of long-term benefit. What cannot be defended is the use of tests that amount to linking a patient's access to life-saving treatment to estimates of social worth, as when the child of unmarried parents is for that reason alone deemed a poor candidate for a heart transplant. Even less supportable is the *de facto* rationing of even routine and readily available care according to the blunt instrument of who has health insurance.

Christian theological premises thus exert a powerful egalitarian pressure on what versions of justice may apply to the distribution of basic social goods like medicine. Libertarian, market-model notions of justice being secured as long as there is no force or fraud are woefully inadequate from a biblical standpoint. The Christian foundation for distributive justice is God's absolute ownership over all Creation and the status of all human "owners" as merely managers of what is God's.

Its foundation for procedural justice is the shared and equal status of all persons as created and called by God. In medicine, they provide a powerful argument for equal access to basic health care whenever absolute scarcity does not make all claims moot.

From Tools to Tasks

In this chapter, we have reviewed the standard principles of bioethics, and given some examples of how they are used to guide and illuminate the practice of medicine. This has included some considera-tion of the perplexities and problems we run into when we try to enact abstract and general duties amid the uncertainties and complexities of real life. We have noted the conflicting interpretations of autonomy, non-maleficence, beneficence and justice that arise out of different understandings of the human situation, and different accounts of human well-being. Finally, we have tried to place these discussions in an explicitly theological context, looking at how these duties are supported or limited or re-cast by central Christian affirmations.

Now it remains to be seen how these principles, appropriately understood and constrained, can work for us as Christians: what clarity or insight they can foster, what sensitivities they can help us to develop, and how they may aid us in speaking and listening to others with whom we must collaborate in our own efforts to care faithfully for the sick and the dying. At the same time, and inevitably, we will be exploring the limitations of these ethical tools—those which arise from the vagaries of their definitions, and those which are inherent in the form of thinking they impose. The most telling way to explore both the contributions and the limits of these tools is to see how they might be applied in particular cases where doubts and disputes arise about the proper course of action.

Chapter 3

Thinking Through Conflicts:
Using Principles in Hard Cases

Real People, Real Decisions

One of the predictable and wrenching problems built into the effort to apply the principles of bioethics to real people and real decisions is that they often come into conflict. No theoretical model can eliminate for us the difficulties, conceptual, moral and emotional, that arise when it seems we must do two incompatible things, or when both of two possible courses of action appear to run head-on into prohibitions. And there are times in caring for the sick when it seems that whatever we do we will be violating our duties—times when we cannot avoid one wrong without committing another. At an intellectual level we can resolve the contradictions rather simply, by reminding ourselves that none of the particular obligations derived from the principles of bioethics is absolute. But this doesn't help us very much. Which of two conflicting principles takes precedence in a particular case of conflict? Or to put it differently, how do we know which of a range of possible responses really does fulfill our obligations to respect the conscience of another, *and* to help and avoid hurting those for whom we wish to care, *and* to respond to the just claims of others?

I have suggested in the preceding chapter that some of these conflicts can be resolved, or at least clarified, when we place these principles into a much wider context: the story of the world and of God's work in it that Christians affirm. And it is true that it helps to see a human life as part of this larger narrative, as itself a story whose final intelligibility is secured by the God who creates, and sustains, and calls it to a close. Sometimes conflicts can be resolved by insights or constraints introduced by the story. A chastened view of what autonomy may authorize, or a broader understanding of moral goods and harms, or a different account of justice—these can help us to recognize when a conflict is more apparent than real. But it would be false and misleading to suggest that this is always possible. No method of thinking through the moral challenges and difficulties of caring for the sick can always eliminate perplexity, assuage doubt, or provide a clear and certain path to avoid the moral and spiritual perils of decisions about life and death. Taking seriously the limitations of our understanding and even of our good will, we must understand all the disciplines of moral thought as efforts to do better rather than worse, rather than as guarantors of clear and certain answers.

Before turning to the consideration of concrete cases, I want to address a matter of the language used in these analyses. Some readers may expect to find among them a discussion of the "quality of life" experienced by patients as a criterion for deciding about treatment. There are two reasons why I do not use that language anywhere in this book. One reason is that the phrase, which is used to some degree by bioethicists and to a greater degree in public and popular discussions, remains ambiguous and vague. It appears to have as many meanings as it has users, including many which are mutually incompatible. Thus, its use seems to me confusing rather than illuminating. In particular, it contributes to an appearance of clarity where clarity does not really exist. Therefore, when I want to talk about the subjective experience of patients as a factor in treatment decisions, I speak instead of the benefits and burdens of treatment or non-treatment, and of the particular interests, hopes, and convictions of patients that color and give meaning to that experience. I think this allows me to consider a rationale for accepting or refusing a given treatment based on the total life experience that will most likely result for the patient, something I am entirely willing to do.

But the other reason I have for avoiding "quality of life" language is its implication that a human life can be comprehensively assessed according to its material possibilities and limitations. I question whether a person's life has a unified or knowable "quality," at least from any perspective other than God's. At any rate, I doubt that it has one that can be understood simply by looking at its balance of pleasant and painful aspects. How do we think about the Stephen Hawkings of the world, or the Helen Kellers, or the unknown children at the local Shriner's Hospital for Crippled Children? How do we understand the lives of the retarded, or the clinically depressed, or the poor, or for that matter anyone whose life is characterized by suffering, whether from illness or loneliness or the spiritual anguish described so vividly by the mystics? I worry that "quality of life" language deflects our attention from outcomes related to treatment. It turns us away from matters of justifying a given intervention to much broader questions about a person's satisfaction with his or her life that may be altogether outside the sphere of medicine. In a culture like ours, where so much is made of happiness and productivity and self-fulfillment, where (philosophical) materialism and empiricism are so dominant, I am frankly afraid of judgments about life's "quality" in a context that has so little room for the depths of human experience. In sum, the language of "quality of life" strikes me, both in theory and often in actual use, as reductionist and potentially dangerous. For these reasons I avoid it as misleading and problematic.

One more thing needs to be said before we try to think through how the principles of bioethics might work in particular situations. The following are real cases, adapted and disguised from the details of actual events, and they give us some taste of the painful decisions that sometimes must be faced, and some glimpse of how we might think about them. But even this is no more than an exercise. There is a literal world of difference between analyzing a case or crafting a position about an "issue," and answering in the moment the question is shouted over the sound of an alarm at the bedside of an aged parent: "Quick! He's stopped breathing! Do I intubate him or let him die?"[1] The starkness of such choices, the pain and fear and grief and guilt that accompany them, and above all the pressure to know and to say right now what ought to be done: all make it seem as if all the detached and comfortable consideration of the study were simply and completely beside the point.

But this too is a mistake, as much of a mistake as it is to suppose that doing one's theoretical homework will eliminate the anguish and uncertainty of real situations. Even if we cannot avoid the necessity of confronting decisions with all the confusions and pressures of life attached, still we can become more thoughtful and more sensitive about what to look for. We can get better at sorting out what can and cannot be accomplished by the courses available to us. We can learn to get beyond the tangle of our emotions, taking seriously what they tell us without assuming that our feelings or our impulses are always secure guides to conduct. And all this is part of the moral capacity that the classical Christian tradition called "prudence": the cultivated ability to see reality truthfully rather than as our desires or our fears would distort it. From this standpoint, all formal methods of moral analysis come down in the end to this: they are tools to help us develop the discipline and clarity to see the world well, and to respond accordingly in love for God and neighbor. It is in this spirit that we will consider how the basic principles of bioethics might help us understand our obligations to the sick.

The Limits of Aggressive Treatment: Intubating the Elderly and Critically Ill

Case #1: Mr. S., a widower 80 years old, has been admitted to the hospital with a diagnosis of bacterial pneumonia confirmed by X-ray. It is his third admission with this diagnosis in two years, and it follows a course of oral antibiotics administered in the nursing home where he resides. Upon admission he has a temperature of 103° and a severe cough, and he complains of generalized pain. He is placed on more powerful intravenous antibiotics and fluids, catheterized due to extreme weakness and debility, and given an oxygen-enriched atmosphere through a mask. In addition, he receives medication for pain and inflammation. After three days of treatment, the fever has climbed to 105°, and the cough has worsened. New chest X-rays reveal that the lungs are slowly filling with fluid. Mr. S. has now become uncommunicative, seeming barely aware of his daughter and son-in-law who visit with him for a few hours every day.

The physician in charge of his case believes that the chances of Mr. S. surviving for any significant period are quite low. He tells the family that "the odds are not good" for recovery, but when questioned acknowledges that he cannot rule out that possibility. After consultation with the patient's daughter, who indicates that she wants to try "anything that might work," the doctor moves Mr. S. to the Intensive Care unit. Mr. S. is experiencing growing difficulty breathing, and his cough is worse. A new antibiotic regimen is begun, and a respiratory therapist comes periodically to suction his lungs, a procedure which appears to cause Mr. S. discomfort, and which he weakly resists. The difficulty in breathing is placing a strain on Mr. S.'s heart, and after two days of respiratory therapy the therapist recommends that they place Mr. S. on a respirator with a tracheal breathing tube. While the doctor and the family are discussing this option, and the patient's overall decline, Mr. S. goes into respiratory arrest. From the bedside the doctor asks the daughter, "Quick! He's stopped breathing. Do I intubate him or let him die?"

✦　✦　✦

Although this may sound like the plot of an over-dramatized TV doctor show, it is in fact the summary of an actual case, altered from the original only in insignificant details. Nor is the story it tells unusual, in which an issue is changed from a topic for discussion into an instant and irreversible decision by a sudden clinical event. This is partly because clinical medicine is full of surprises, but also it is partly because we are, all of us, generally reluctant to translate our thinking about sickness and death into decisions before that task is forced upon us by events.

This case raises a number of issues, from the vagaries of determining mental status and competence, to the nature of the physician's role as patient advocate, to the role and character of hope in the process of medical decision-making. It also illustrates something of the way in which issues which are conceptually distinct become mingled and related when they are encountered in real life. Particularly, the distinction between substantive questions (What should be done?) and procedural questions (Who should decide?) is often less clear in practice than it may be in theory.

One way of looking at the case involves thinking about the potential decision-makers, and their respective claims and obligations. Initially Mr. S. is weak and ill but conscious, and able at least to assent to his own treatment. At this point he clearly has the right, founded in autonomy, to accept or refuse any kind of treatment. His acceptance of admission and intravenous antibiotics may fairly be interpreted as an expression of hope and desire that treatment might resolve the pneumonia this time as it had in the past.

When Mr. S. becomes uncommunicative and appears not to be fully aware of his surroundings, the physician turns to the adult daughter for decisions about ongoing treatment. This is because, by law and custom, the next-of-kin has the primary role in treatment decisions *if and when* a patient is unable to make decisions for him/herself. This policy reflects both respect for the autonomy of families as fundamental social groups, and the expectation that close relatives are best able to determine and most committed to serving the interests of patients (beneficence). This authority is not unlimited, however. It is constrained on the one hand by the patient's previously expressed wishes, and on the other by the patient's basic interests.

Finally, the physician has obligations to his patient (grounded in respect for autonomy) to respect his wishes, and those of the family as substitutes when the patient cannot speak for himself. However, he also has a duty to serve the patient's best interest by exercising his clinical skill and judgment to recommend the best course (beneficence), as well as a duty to prevent unnecessary harm. In extreme cases, where a patient's clear interests are being violated, it may even be a doctor's obligation to seek legal intervention to override familial decisions for or against treatment. Such an intervention would be based on the physician's duty not to harm by medical means, and on the patient's claim not to be unfairly burdened by mistreatment or neglect (nonmaleficence and justice).

Assuming that Mr. S. really is incapable of forming and communicating his own preferences about treatment,[2] the relevant question for both the treatment team and the daughter making decisions on her father's behalf becomes, "What course of treatment will best serve his interests?" In language a little less detached, it becomes a question of what they should do to care for and keep faith with one so acutely ill. The answer depends partly upon an assessment of what the available treatments are, what hardships they will impose upon the patient, and how likely they are to bring about significant improvement. Such assessments must be informed by the skill and clinical experience of the hospital staff, both doctors and nurses. Their careful and considered judgments about what can reasonably be expected from a given course of treatment are crucial factors in understanding what kind of care is respectful, helpful and just. These professional judgments must be communicated gently but also clearly, with appropriate humility but without disingenuous "hopefulness" that exaggerates the chances for success. To do otherwise only confuses or deceives families already struggling with the temptation to deny what seems too painful to face.

But the answer to what treatment constitutes faithful care for Mr. S. depends as well upon some kind of evaluation of different possible outcomes and what they will mean for the patient. If, for example, the family knows that Mr. S. has a great personal stake in even a short period of life extension, then even a low probability of offering such extension makes a treatment more attractive. If, conversely, the family has reason to believe that Mr. S. will find the invasion and discomfort of treatment terribly burdensome, then that may shift the balance of possible benefits and harms away from the most aggressive therapies. The point is just that the general duties of non-maleficence and beneficence take their particular content from the things which are important to the patient, the goals and plans and concerns and commitments which animate him.

To adopt another and more comprehensive language: The shape taken by our efforts to avoid harm and to do good depends partly on how different events will be incorporated into the story of someone's life. What character they have depends on how they can be made sense of in light of that story. This means that the goods and harms considered in treatment must be considered as they arise for that patient, in light of that person's loves and fears and hopes and convictions, and those of the community where this life is lived and cherished and interpreted. For this is the wider context in which all life experience is to be understood, and where human events have their meaning. They are not "objective" and abstract gains and losses which can be read and understood, as it were, in isolation and from the outside.

From a Christian standpoint, both illness and recovery, both improvement and decline, both survival and death, are capable of being taken up into the story of a life lived in God's care and service. In turn, a life story with any of these elements can be taken up into the larger story of the community of faith where it has its place and intelligibility. This does not mean that the outcome is a matter of indifference. But it does mean that within the Christian community, all the events of a human life must be considered as part of a story that includes mortality, and one that can affirm the trustworthiness of God in and beyond death. If all of Christian life is vocation, God's call to service, then death too must be seen as a call. It is neither to be sought as an escape from suffering, nor to be avoided at any cost as an evil which places us beyond the reach of God's mercy.[3]

Finally, in this case, where the burdens of treatment are considerable and its likely benefits limited in time and scope, questions of justice arise. Spaces in an Intensive Care Unit are almost always a scarce life-saving resource. Seeing all human lives as God's entails considering the effects of treatment decisions on other lives, including lives for whom the benefits conferred by the same resources might be much clearer and greater. For all these reasons, a Christian construal of the principles of bioethics suggests (without flatly entailing) that care for this patient may now take the form of withholding further invasive measures, and allowing death to ensue. This is emphatically not a matter of "giving up hope," but rather of placing one's hope in a good larger and more enduring than forestalling death.

The Limits of Aggressive Treatment: Surgery for the Very Premature Infant

Case #2: A 24-year-old woman, 25 weeks pregnant with her first child, arrives at the hospital already in labor. Medication to delay labor is given, as well as a steroid injection to speed the development of the fetal lungs, in case delivery cannot be postponed. Some twenty-four hours after admission, and before the steroids can have any effect, the amniotic sack breaks and labor cannot be stopped. Within two hours, an infant, a boy weighing 760 grams (1 lb .11 oz.), is born. He does not breathe spontaneously upon delivery. The parents ask the attending pediatricians, specialists in newborn care, to do all that they can to save the life of their premature baby, who is at the borderline of viability.

It takes the team ten minutes to resuscitate the infant, and his heart must be stimulated to beat. He requires maximum ventilator support, with a tracheal tube and a highly oxygen-enriched atmosphere. Too small and weak to take fluids by mouth, he is supported by intravenous feeding. For one week the infant remains fairly stable in the Newborn Intensive Care Unit. He suffers weight loss, jaundice, and other problems associated with prematurity, but there is no indication of brain hemorrhaging or other immediately life-threatening conditions. However, on the ninth day, blood gas tests show that insufficient oxygen is reaching the blood stream. It seems that the lungs, immature and fragile at best, are now being further damaged by the intrusion of the ventilator tube and the high-pressure air delivered by the respirator. Increasing the pressure risks tearing a hole in the lungs: on the other hand, prolonged oxygen starvation will certainly cause further damage to the brain and other organs. If he does survive, it will be with respiratory disease due to lung scarring, and with an unpredictable degree of damage to the brain and other organs caused by oxygen insufficiency. Preparing to increase ventilator pressure, doctors ask the parents' permission to insert a chest tube surgically if the increased pressure tears the lungs.

✦　✦　✦

Cases like this one are quite common in large American cities, where there is immediate access to a specialized intensive care technology that is as daunting as it is dazzling. In hospitals like the one in this case, fully equipped Newborn Intensive Care Units (NICUs) can sometimes sustain the lives of infants born as little as 24 weeks from conception, not far past the half-way point in the 40-week human gestation period. The intoxicating possibility, compelling to physicians and even more powerful to the desperate parents of sick or premature infants, is of rescuing an infant on the very edge of viability and restoring him or her to a whole life. This possibility is brought home to physicians and parents alike by the common practice of having all the "graduates" of an NICU gather for an annual celebration of the lives of these children who would not have survived without this dramatic form of care.

But wed to the possibility of saving the smallest and sickest patients are two others: the possibility (indeed, the probability) of protracting the dying process and inflicting increased suffering on many infants who cannot be saved; and the possibility of sustaining for some a level of functioning that is so minimal and fraught with such difficulty and pain that one would not choose it for oneself or a loved one, even if death were the only alternative. Very few infants born before 25 weeks gestation will survive without serious and permanent disabilities, ranging from blindness and deafness to massive brain damage and all its effects. And the prognosis of infants like this one who have been oxygen-deprived for more than ten minutes at birth is similarly grim. But the agonizing reality is that, much of the time, even the best diagnosis and the most sophisticated techniques cannot predict whether recovery, or prolongation of death, or survival with massive and devastating problems will result—not in time to guide decisions about how aggressively to treat. The obligations of care givers not to cause harm and suffering are here brought into maximum tension with their commitment to sustain life and heal injury.

If we try to think of this case in terms of the duties to respect autonomy, avoid harm, provide benefit and treat all persons justly, we learn first what questions need to be asked. In order to ensure that treatment decisions are a real exercise of the parents' judgment, and that they can serve the interests of the infant whose life or death depends upon them, we need the best information that can be given. How difficult is the proposed surgery itself? How likely is it that this infant will survive even with the surgery? What will be his prospects for eventual weaning from the respirator if the surgery is successful? On another front, how severe will be the brain damage if he does survive? Such information can usually be only statistical in nature: the child has an X% chance of survival overall; the surgery is successful in Y% of patients; the degree of predictable brain damage falls somewhere in a range from Q to Z.

None of this can resolve the uncertainties for *this* child here and now. And all of the predictions may fail, leaving an outcome much better or much worse than anyone anticipated. But if the duties of parents and care givers are to avoid harm and to do good, then decision-makers cannot avoid weighing what is possible, what is likely, and what we are able to discern as serving the child's well-being. They are left to play a sort of desperate game of odds, and most of the "what if" questions that haunt them can never be resolved. The only justification for making decisions amid such obscurity is necessity. We cannot know what the outcome will be, yet decisions must and will be made, either by our actions or our inaction.

In these situations of terrible uncertainty, a great deal of latitude is generally given to parental autonomy. Physicians are very reluctant either to begin or to end treatment without the consent and support of the parents, who will have to live with the results of either course of action. (Although there have been a number of well-publicized cases in which physicians and parents have gone to court to resolve conflicts over whether or not to treat a very sick or premature newborn, these are very much the exceptions and not the rule.) While this attention to the judgment of parents is appropriate, it also places parents struggling with shock, grief and fear in a brutally difficult position. They are charged with making life and death decisions for their newborn children about medical conditions and treatment possibilities they cannot hope fully to understand.

Nor can we ever forget that while the parents are generally the decision-makers, the infant is the patient, and the one to whom care givers *and* parents have duties to help and not to harm. Thus, amid the unknowns of treatment, caught between the desire to save and the desire not to inflict pointless misery, parents are faced with another kind of challenge as well. Bound up with their need to weigh the goods and harms of treatment is the need to ask searching questions about the meaning of physical wholeness or handicap; to look deeply into their own understanding of the place of suffering in human life; and to look long and hard at their own motives and intentions as they try to decide what is best for their children.

To engage in such reflection as a Christian is to begin with the presumption that all human lives are "broken" in various ways. Christians affirm that our welcoming of and loyalty toward one another within the Christian community is based not on our capacities and achievements, not on our "wholeness" or wellness at all but rather spectacularly on our un-wellness, on our common flight to the only One who can restore us to health and wholeness.

Moreover, to take seriously our status as creatures is to recognize that the attachments between family members are not simply chosen, but reflect part of the givenness of human life. It is to acknowledge that humans come into existence already in relation, with dependencies and duties derived from the created nature of humans as social and sexual beings. To weigh these duties as Christians is also to begin with a disposition to think of others before ourselves, and to recognize that the deepest and most distinctively human goods in life depend on our willingness to bear the burdens of our connection to one another. The freedom to which Christians are called is genuine and important, but it is freedom *for* rather than *from* each other. And a concept of justice formed by the Christian story will always include a pressure toward universality, and a tendency to defend the welfare of the smallest, the weakest, the least "valuable" of society's members, as we recall that "to such belong God's kingdom."

Reflections like these do not lead with any sort of inevitability to one conclusion or another. It is not to be imagined that loyalty to our desperately sick offspring will always or even usually take the form of pursuing the maximum possible medical intervention. There *have* been cases where parents have refused uncomplicated and clearly life-saving treatment simply because they did not want to accept a child who would not be "normal." But there have also been cases where parents insisted that "everything be done" not because further aggressive treatment held out any real benefit for their child, but because they themselves were unable or unwilling to face the reality of death. It is easy to sympathize with parents torn in either of these ways; nonetheless, we must recognize decisions made on the basis of such parental desires and fears for the temptations that they are.

As unsatisfying a conclusion as it is, and as fraught with dangers, there is simply no better guide to what to do in such a case than this: the obligations of parents and care givers (non-maleficence, beneficence, and justice) converge in the responsibility to choose the course that, according to the best information available to them, seems most to serve the interests and the well-being of the child. These are not, of course, wholly distinct from those of the parents, but neither are they wholly absorbed in them. The role of parent and the role of physician both require that the child's needs and claims have priority where they conflict with those of others.

This means that the parents' natural desire for a healthy child cannot dictate that this infant be neglected or eliminated: this is their child, and he must be cared for, even if that care sometimes rightly takes the form of ending treatment. It also means that extraneous factors like the care givers' fears of malpractice litigation cannot determine what treatment decisions they accept or protest. And it requires that the realistic benefits and burdens of treatment be estimated and weighed as nearly as possible from the viewpoint of the infant. If the proposed surgery and the continued treatment it makes possible provides some reasonable hope of a life not wholly submerged in the struggle for minimal survival; if its pain and difficulty (which are known) do not outweigh that hope, then surgery should be chosen. If none of those conditions apply, then aggressive treatment ought to be ended, and replaced by care aimed at keeping the child free of pain and giving him all the human comfort he is able to receive until his death.

It would be pointless and cruel to minimize the anguish or the bitterness of such choices, or to suggest that Christian faith will or should allow parents to face them with equanimity. Faith in such circumstances is no more than final confidence in a mercy that is hidden from view, and the trust that God does not abandon us in our grief, rage and perplexity. It does not shield us from pain or tragedy, but only promises the companionship of One who has gone before us in suffering: One in whom, in some unfathomable way, all will finally be well.

Artificial Feeding and Futility: Treating a Stroke Victim

Case #3: Mrs. G., a widow 64 years old, is admitted to the hospital after a stroke of moderate severity. Within a few days, she regains consciousness and her vital functions are stable. By the end of two weeks, she has recovered some of the muscle control on the affected side. However, she remains unable to speak intelligibly and her mental status is unclear. In addition, feeding is difficult and her appetite remains poor. Mrs. G. does not have a living will, nor has she appointed a person to make medical decisions on her behalf. After consultation with the family, a gastronomy tube is placed to provide full nutritional support.

During this period, she is visited regularly by her son and his family, her only remaining relatives. She sometimes appears glad to see them, and seems to enjoy their hugs and other gestures of affection. However, they do not believe she knows who they are. After a short time of visiting, her attention seems to wander and she appears to forget that they are there. Much of her waking time is spent simply staring at the walls of her room. When there is no observable change in her by the end of the sixth week, the family asks the physician whether Mrs. G. will ever recover fully from her stroke, and they are told "probably not." The family then asks the hospital whether they might end the artificial feeding, since her condition does not appear to be improving, and continued treatment appears to them to be futile.

✦　✦　✦

Like all cases involving the question of whether artificial feeding (by intravenous drip, naso-gastric tube, or gastronomy tube) can rightly be ended, this case brings out deep and powerful emotional responses. On one hand, we normally recoil from the idea of letting a person die of starvation and dehydration when we have the means to provide her with nourishment. After all, food and water are the most basic of necessities, common to all life, and the need for them is not the result of disease but of normal function. On the other hand, when the state of existence that is preserved for a patient by these means is one of minimal experience or even of no conscious experience at all, it is easy to ask the question, "Why are we doing this?" Precisely because we have powerful but often conflicting moral intuitions about such cases, it will be helpful to think through the reasons which might be given for withholding medically provided food and water. Then we will be in a position to consider how best to care for Mrs. G.

Questions about whether artificial nutrition and hydration may ever be withdrawn reach their most acute form in two kinds of cases: one is when artificial feeding sustains the life of a person who is permanently unconscious, having irrevocably lost the brain functions that support awareness. A second set of issues arises when the provision of artificial feeding seems only to prolong a difficult dying, extending a period of suffering that would otherwise be shortened by the inability to take regular nourishment. Although death by dehydration or starvation is not painless or easy, it is not necessarily worse than all other ways of dying. It is arguable that lengthening by artificial nutrition the life of someone who is inexorably dying of something as painful as bone cancer imposes a burden unmatched by any benefit.

These two scenarios differ in one significant respect. In the first one, artificial feeding for a permanently unconscious patient is questioned because the treatment seems to offer no benefit to that patient. In the second, such feeding is questioned because it imposes a burden on a patient by prolonging a painful dying. Both of these considerations are directly related to the duties of beneficence and non-maleficence, since these are understood as matters of balancing the benefits and harms caused by medical treatment. If care givers are to perform only those procedures that, on balance, help and do not harm the patient, then both kinds of argument must be seriously considered.

It is not obvious from a medical standpoint, nor has it ever been the conclusion from the Christian standpoint, that one must do anything and everything one can to preserve life for as long as possible in all circumstances. However, the Christian conviction that God is sovereign over life has traditionally been understood to mean that one must not aim at death: that to do so is to intend an evil, even if only as a means to a good end such as relieving suffering. One of the most consistent and strongest objections to ending artificial nutrition for patients has been the recognition that such a course will make death inevitable, quite apart from the course of any underlying disease or injury. A patient who is not provided food and water *will* die, and will die as a direct result of that decision, unless some other condition causes death first. Does that mean that a decision to withhold artificial feeding from a patient who cannot eat must indeed intend death, aim at it whether as end or means? Or can medically provided nutrition sometimes be ended because of the burdens it imposes (fear and anxiety, the need for restraints, recurrent infections, pulmonary edema, cardiac stress, or prolonging pain)? Is it possible to regard it as an unwarranted invasion of the body when in sustaining only vegetative functions, it maintains metabolism without making possible any of the things for the sake of which metabolism is maintained?

If these can be persuasive reasons for ending medical nutrition and hydration, then in the first case the aim of withdrawing artificial feeding would be to eliminate the fears, discomforts and physical injuries imposed by that form of treatment. Death would be foreseen as the result, but not willed. (Thus if the patient were to recover the ability to eat without the bodily invasion of artificial feeding, it would be good news, not a frustration of the intended outcome of death.) For a permanently unconscious patient, the aim would be to stop the indignity of invading the body for the sake of a treatment which could no longer offer the patient any benefit. This depends upon accepting the notion that the physiological functions that can be sustained by means of artificial feeding are no benefit to the patient after the possibility of consciousness has been lost. Again death would be foreseen, but accepted as the outcome rather than actively willed.

These are difficult judgments, to be made with fear and trembling, and a vivid sense of the moral and spiritual perils that accompany them. It is and ought to be a fearsome thing to embark on a course of action which will certainly result in a patient's death. Still, because of the invasive and sometimes burdensome nature of the means used to provide long-term artificial nutrition, there are good reasons to regard it as optional *under some circumstances*. This is to concur with the recent trend in court decisions and public policy deliberations which treat such interventions as medical treatments which may in some cases *not* be in a patient's interest. With this discussion in mind, we are now ready to return to the matter of what kind of care we owe Mrs. G.

The first thing to be noted in the present case is that neither of the persuasive objections to artificial feeding—that it may place great burdens *on the patient* and that it may sometimes not offer any real benefit *to the patient*—apply here. Mrs. G. is not struggling to remove a feeding tube, and is not terrified and distressed by physical restraints used to keep such a tube in place. She is not apparently suffering great pain or other distress. Neither is she in a state of unconsciousness, unaware of her environment and beyond the reach of human companionship and care. It is said that she sometimes seems glad to see her relatives, and that she seems to enjoy their embraces, even if she cannot identify them or communicate with them due to the effects of her stroke. This is a long way from being completely deprived of experience, and also a long way from being unaffected by the physical suffering of dehydration and starvation that would result if artificial feeding were ended. As reduced as the sphere of her life has become, and as emotionally painful as it may be for her family to continue to see her with her abilities and her personality shrouded in the fog of a damaged brain, she is not faced with intractable suffering. Nor is hers the vacuum of experience created by the permanent destruction of all awareness.

The crucial thing about the arguments for ending artificial feeding even when it is certain that death will result is that the weighing of benefits and burdens is done *from the patient's standpoint*. This is crucial because, in the case of the great majority of patients who have not communicated their wishes for or against such treatment, the first obligation of care givers and family is to protect the interests of persons who are utterly helpless to protect themselves. From Mrs. G.'s standpoint, the burdens imposed by artificial feeding do not appear to be very great, at least at the present where there is no evidence of the physical problems such feeding can cause. At the same time, there are significant benefits for her. These are both positive in the sense of prolonging a life that includes some degree of awareness and of satisfaction, and negative in the sense of averting a painful and difficult death by dehydration and starvation.

Artificial feeding might be called "futile" in this case from the standpoint of one looking for a cure or full recovery from the stroke; but in terms of an expression of human care and comfort, and as a means of supporting even a circumscribed existence, it is not futile at all. In short, although the continued provision of artificial nutrition for

Mrs. G. places real stress on the family, and creates real financial and practical demands on the wider society, these are offset by the genuine benefits it provides for a helpless patient. Therefore, this is a reasonable course of treatment in which benefits for the patient outweigh burdens on the patient, and the obligations of non-maleficence and beneficence require us to provide it. Our willingness to provide such care for the unproductive, and to remain present with one another even in the face of the painful losses of disease and disability, is part of our imitation and embodiment of God's faithfulness to us even in the face of weakness and limitation. It reflects our determination to care even when we cannot cure, even as it requires that we sustain both courage and humility in the face of inevitable decline.

Choosing Death: Food Refusal as a Means of "Self-Deliverance"

Case #4: Mrs. E., 85 years old and widowed some years ago, has experienced an escalating series of health problems over the last six months including severe diarrhea, rectal prolapse, anemia, and an irregular heartbeat. These have left her weak, achy, without bowel and bladder control, and with rapidly failing eyesight. She is now bedridden, and must live in a nursing home, a situation she had desperately wished to avoid. Her prognosis makes it clear that she has no prospect of recovering sufficient health to return to the independent life she had cherished. Moreover, she is now unable to engage in the hobbies and activities she used to enjoy, walking and reading. On the other hand, none of her conditions is life-threatening.

Facing this limited and dependent existence, Mrs. E. decides that she wishes to die. Her adult sons and daughter, one of whom has lived next door for years, talk with her at some length over a period of several weeks, during which she expresses her sense of humiliation and despair over the loss of control over her own life, and her desire to end it by her own decision before she experiences further decline and dependency. Her children come reluctantly to support her in this desire, on the ground that she is well-informed, stable, and not depressed. She asks her doctor for help, requesting that he set up a morphine drip which she could increase to a lethal dose. He explains that such an act would be illegal. Mrs. E. is frustrated by this refusal, considering laws against suicide and euthanasia an unwarranted intrusion into private decisions. She and her adult children discuss other strategies for suicide, including prescription drug overdose and methods of self-asphyxiation. In the end, Mrs. E. contracts pneumonia and refuses antibiotic treatment. Finally, when the pneumonia shows signs of abating on its own, Mrs. E. refuses food and water. Six days later she dies, having expressed nothing but satisfaction with her ability to end her life as she chose.[4]

✦ ✦ ✦

The aspects of this case that bear discussion do not chiefly have to do with what was actually done by the various participants, or with the final outcome. It seems clear enough that the physician who refuses actively to end his patient's life is acting at least with reasonable prudence by citing laws against assisted suicide and euthanasia. It is also clear that Mrs. E. is within her rights to refuse first antibiotics and finally food and water, whether ordinary or artificial in their delivery. The right to refuse any and all kinds of medical treatment is guaranteed to competent patients by the requirement of informed consent, the foremost expression of autonomy, and there are few circumstances that would justify force-feeding a competent patient. It can be argued that everyone in this story does what they are permitted to do, and that the result is a happy one for all parties: Mrs. E. is able to regain control over what happens to her, even to choose her own dying; her adult children feel that they have supported her in achieving her goals; and the hospital staff is able passively to permit rather than actively to cause Mrs. E.'s death.

In some sense, it is not narrowly in the realm of medical ethics that this case is challenging or controversial. For what is remarkable in it is not the treatments that are used or withheld, which are quite routine. What is notable is not the use or non-use of medicine at all, but rather the understandings of human existence and of human choice, presumed by all sides, that drive the decisions which are made. These are partly played out in the arena of medicine, in that they come to define the ends medicine is given to serve. Medical intervention (or its refusal) is taken as a means to end suffering, and suffering is defined to include whatever the individual patient finds unacceptable. Mrs. E., after all, is experiencing discomfort and weakness, not intractable pain. She is unable to walk and to live independently, but she is able to think, or to talk, or to enjoy her family. She can still appreciate music or poetry readings or any number of other intellectual, aesthetic, and emotional outlets. Her sphere of activity is reduced, certainly; it is hardly contracted to nothing. This is not to detract in the slightest from the sympathy that we ought to have for Mrs. E., who is experiencing real and important losses which she naturally grieves. Her pain and despair are genuine and important in themselves. It is simply to try to make a distinction between her situation and that of patients whose losses are more nearly total, and whose pain is desperate and unrelenting.

There are cases in which we are unable to alleviate a patient's great suffering, cases in which continued existence itself seems an enormous struggle and an unimaginable burden. We rightly agonize over what constitutes compassion in such circumstances, and over the apparent cruelty of what is meant as care. Cases like these test the limits of human responsibility and human endurance, and they challenge our understanding of the aims and limits of medicine. But this is not such a case. One might say that in this case the notion that the outcomes of treatment are to be weighed in terms of a particular patient's hopes and desires and fears is taken to its logical extreme. The goal of medicine is understood to be something like "life-satisfaction."

Beyond even this redefinition of medicine, the crucial aspect of this case is that it is Mrs. E.'s own experience, especially her interpretation of what is happening to her as her health declines, which determines everything else. Presumably it is because they accept Mrs. E.'s own understanding of her situation that her children and the medical personnel acquiesce in her desire to die even though her physical condition is neither desperately painful nor fatal.

The most obvious and striking aspect of that understanding is the assumed right of self-disposal. It should be borne in mind that what Mrs. E. rejects is not invasive and burdensome therapy, but ordinary food and water. It is not excessive medical treatment, but the conditions of her life that are a burden to her. This is not a case about treatment refusal, but one about the acceptability of suicide as a response to a non-fatal illness and its associated disability. Mrs. E. takes for granted that her life is hers to continue or to end as she sees fit, at a time of her own choosing and for whatever reasons seem good to her. The notion that the wider society should have any stake in her life, or any say about what she may do to end it, seems both to surprise and to offend her. Even her own children are included in her decision only to the extent of her presenting her reasons for her decision, and seeking their support in achieving her goal. In fact Mrs. E. has no dependents in either a material or an emotional sense, no one who is relying on her for basic support, and there is no obvious question of justice posed by her desire to die. It might have made a difference if there had been. As it is, the worth or significance of her life, and thus the rational choice of when to end it, is taken to be a matter of exclusively private judgment.

In calling this attitude remarkable, I am of course speaking from the standpoint of Christian faith, which makes quite contrary assumptions about the "ownership" of human existence. In fact, it may well be the case that Mrs. E. represents the dominant attitude in our own society. Since we do not share a religious or philosophical or even a civic ideal to provide us with the measure of a worthwhile life, it may even be inevitable that we fall back on a rather vacuous "freedom to choose" as the only common good we can recognize. In such a context, suicide may logically be seen as "the ultimate individual right,"[5] the final expression of autonomy. The contrast with a Christian view, which proceeds from the assumption that life is both a gift and a trust for whose use we are accountable to God and to a community of others, is very clear.

But this assumption about the scope and privacy of autonomous choice is only one of the remarkable aspects of this story. The other is the way in which Mrs. E. experiences ill health and the physical limitation and dependency it enforces as a reason for despair, and even for seeking death. On the face of it, it seems surprising that a woman with a loving and attentive family, and with the personal and material resources to provide a stimulating and pleasant environment, should find her existence intolerable. A clue to this assessment may be found in her expressed sense of humiliation at not being in control of her own life.

What Mrs. E. seems to fear, what is to her literally a fate worse than death, might be thought to be an existence deprived of the activities in which she finds pleasure. But this cannot be the full explanation, for she makes no attempt to pursue medical or other options which might restore some of her enjoyment, such as audio-taped books, a colostomy to deal with her incontinence, or a motorized wheel chair to restore the mobility she prized. Even more basically she seems to dread an existence over which she cannot exercise control, in which she simply suffers the constraints of her bodily limitations and her resultant dependence on other people without being able to determine what happens to her. Such a loss of independence is, to her, a humiliation, a basic violation of what it is to be human. It is her own physical and mental decline that Mrs. E. is unwilling to endure, rather than any particular restriction, preferring instead a death which she does not suffer but rather elects.

In short, for Mrs. E. it is independent agency that seems finally to be the measure of a tolerable human existence. This reflects the modern assumption that human dignity consists in the ability to choose and control one's own reality, rather than in the grace to live a human and humane life within the limits of a given physical reality (including the limits of embodiment and mortality). It seems a rather thin account. One might think that Mrs. E. has sold herself short, not prizing as she might the mental and emotional capacities that she still displays even in her pursuit of her own death. Nor does she view the enjoyment and the significance her life might bring to others, such as her children and grandchildren, or the loss to them caused by her death, as a sufficient reason to endure the limitations she finds so disheartening.

Having said all of this, it remains to be observed that on its own terms, the reasoning behind this story of choosing death rather than enduring illness and decline is coherent and perfectly intelligible. It simply reflects a widely held secular understanding of the character and the ends of human existence, one compassed by the pursuit of individual and personally chosen satisfactions, from which the individual may choose to retire when these satisfactions disappear. But such a focus on human agency and control as the essential and humanizing characteristics of existence is problematic from a Christian standpoint in a number of ways.

To begin with, it seems to restrict full humanity to the adult, healthy, able-bodied, adequately fed and sheltered portions of the human population who do not live under conditions of oppression or deprivation: that is, to that minority which can exercise a significant degree of personal autonomy. In addition, it depends upon an understanding of human existence as fundamentally individual and independent, rather than as fundamentally structured by membership in the community and as fundamentally dependent upon God. From the perspective of basic Christian affirmations, such a human self-under-standing is illusory, and distorts the nature of our existence. It lacks a full appreciation of the contingency of creaturely existence, and the intrinsically social character of moral life.

As a result, the particular forms of humility and patience which would have precluded such a choice are underdeveloped. To put it differently, the ability to find fulfillment in living with and for others even under the reality of suffering is the work of grace, grace which is formed in us by the reception of life with all its limitations as the good gift of a loving God. Mrs. E. clearly displays a certain kind of courage in her willingness to face death. However, she does not evidence courage of another kind which is finally deeper and more necessary to human life as Christians understand it: the courage to live within limits not of her own choosing. As Christian participants in a wider society we may need to accept such decisions as falling within the sphere of protected individual liberty; we need not praise them as heroic, nor hold them up as the fullest expression of human dignity.

The Usefulness of Cases

There are, of course, dozens of other current issues and cases which might be discussed, involving advanced reproductive technologies or organ transplants or the use of genetic manipulation. The preceding, more pedestrian, examples were chosen for their representation of perennial and predictable questions that arise in the course of routine care: questions about the limits of aggressive treatment, the basis of decisions to treat handicapped infants, and the issues that surround termination or refusal of life support for elderly patients. These are issues that the average practicing pastor or hospital chaplain may expect to see again and again, as new techniques create new variations on old questions about the ends and the limits of medicine.[6]

That there is a significant amount of overlap in the various cases is no surprise. In part it is a reflection of the method of mapping individual cases against the four general obligations articulated by the principles of bioethics. Beyond that, it is a testimony to the features shared by hard cases, in which basic claims and duties exist in a tension with one another which cannot be wholly resolved. But the details of each individual case give us some taste of how the same concerns—

weighing the effects of treatment, giving patients and families clear and honest information on which to base decisions, listening to the fears and desires of patients, attending to the needs and claims of others—take on different characters as patients are old or young, participating or incompetent, struggling to live or asking to die. They give us a chance to practice with principles as tools, as guides to what questions we ought to ask, even in all the many cases where they cannot provide us with definitive answers.

Finally, cases like these give us some opportunity to see how differing starting points give distinctive content and direction to general obligations like respecting autonomy or avoiding harm. They help us to see what difference it makes in our reasoning and reflection if we accept as true the story of human life and its place in God's world that Christians tell. This will be some modest help to us as we turn to the tasks of reflection and discernment which form part of the pastor's role in helping patients and families face dilemmas in treatment.

Chapter 4

Discernment and Witness:
The Roles of the Pastor in Medical Crisis

Perhaps the initial feeling common to ministers coming into a hospital or other clinical setting to visit a parishioner is that of being out of place. A hospital has a peculiar kind of apartness, a quality of being a universe unto itself that comes of being in fact a kind of micro-society. It is a world into which the whole range of human experience is compressed. Not only are people being born and dying here; they are also eating and sleeping and cooking and cleaning and playing and socializing here, in fact performing the thousands of activities that are necessary to sustain a *de facto* community of hundreds or thousands through twenty-four hours of every day. They are doing it day in and day out, in every kind of weather and every season, through holidays and summer vacations, in the midst of national tragedies and celebrations, in many ways unaffected by the rhythms and events of life outside the hospital walls. Patterns as basic as day and night lose their significance here. Even in those small towns where activity seems to cease at nightfall, the emergency room and the delivery room are open, the pharmacy and the surgical suites continue in operation, indeed sometimes become busier due to whatever force makes fevers rise and medical crises intensify in the middle of the night.

There are also a number of powerful social cues that work to divide people present in a hospital into those who belong there, and those who are just passing through. Uniforms and the ubiquitous pocket badges, white lab coats and the stethoscopes that dangle like talismans around the necks of doctors and nurses, all identify those who belong. The sure footsteps of those who know precisely where they are going (and have been there a thousand times) contrast with the tentative steps and confused expressions of visitors and those whose business with the hospital is limited and occasional. Unfortunately, even the patients for whose sake the whole edifice is supposed to exist often feel like

outsiders, interruptions in the round of hurried and obviously important activities that fill the days of hospital personnel. In such a setting,
it is very easy for the chaplain or the visiting pastor to feel nothing so
much as beside the point.

But for all the concentrated and specialized knowledge represented
by the staff of a hospital, for all of the genuinely dazzling skills
possessed by its physicians and nurses and support staff, there is
conferred no special expertise in living. No transcendent insight into
what we're all doing here is conveyed by proximity to the dramatic
moments of birth and death. To use the old distinction expressed easily
in Greek, the modern hospital is a triumph of *techné*, the technical skill
that fits means to ends; but as often as not, it is also a standing cry for
sophrosuné, the more fundamental wisdom that knows what ends are
worth pursuing, and why. The questions that trouble the consciences
and disturb the sleep of sensitive and compassionate practitioners of
medicine are very often familiar and even ancient questions: "How do
we know this is all worthwhile?"; or even "If a man dies, shall he live
again?" (Job 14:14). In such things there are no experts, not among
doctors and nurses, and no more among pastors and theologians. But
these are the questions which are the birth of all religion, and the
answers we give to them *are* the substance of our diverse faiths, whether
their language be overtly theological or not. In short, this is familiar
terrain for theological reflection, and country in which the pastor can
be very much at home.

Moreover, it is a place where the pastor can offer patients and
families a chance to reclaim their own experience from the efficient
alienness of the hospital. She or he can offer a conversation and a
language which may enable patients and their families to affirm that
"none of us lives or dies to himself alone" (Rom. 14:7), and to bring
this experience back into a framework where it can be interpreted and
shared by a community of faith.

The Ministry of Presence

The single essential aspect of pastoral care for the sick and the
suffering is as mundane and as necessary as bread: it is simply presence.
Before and after anything else one may need to do or say, more crucial

than any advice that might be offered or any service that might be performed, the minister fulfills her or his commission to serve the people of God just by being and remaining with those who are sick or dying. Obviously, being present is the precondition to any other kind of ministry, but the point here is rather that being present is itself an active and vital ministry. It is nothing less than the evidence and the embodiment of the presence of Christ who is with us in his body the church. And when we face the isolation and self-alienation of illness, when the bodies we think of as "ours" or even as "us" appear to us as objects and adversaries, we need to experience the presence of God in the most concrete fashion: in the flesh.

Madeleine L'Engle tells a story about her young son, and of her husband's effort late one evening to get the child settled in bed and ready for sleep. Father and son had gone through the standard round of bedtime stories and prayers and drinks of water, followed by some special requests for extra hugs and favorite stuffed animals. Over many repetitions the father's patience was wearing thin, until he was touched by the child's admission, "I'm just feeling lonesome." Searching for a reassurance that would let the boy fall asleep peacefully (and also allow him to return to other tasks), her husband reminded his son that he was not alone, for God was always with him. "Yes, I know," said the boy, "but I need someone with skin on."[1] The Incarnation is God's testimony to the fact that we *all* need someone with skin on, and never more so than when we confront the loneliness of illness, and the ultimate and irreducible individuality of death.

This insistence upon presence as an aspect of ministry, obvious as it is, needs such emphasis because there are countervailing forces which make it difficult for pastors to be present with the sick and the dying. Likewise, it may be difficult for those facing illness to accept the gifts of time and companionship even from this, the community's "official" representative. As a result, ministers frequently offer no more than a token "visit" of five or ten uncomfortable minutes at the end of which it is hard to tell who is more relieved, visitor or visited. This may be adequate for a patient whose hospital stay is more or less brief and routine, who may be expected to return promptly to the worshiping community and for whom this represents no more than an uncomfortable interruption in ordinary life. But it is far from adequate for the patient suffering from serious or prolonged illness, and still less so for the patient who must face the imminence of death and the need to make decisions about what kind of treatment makes sense.

The first difficulty in being with parishioners who are hospitalized is the one already mentioned, the minister's sense of being out of place and irrelevant. In the last fifty years, we have seen the development of so much capacity to intervene in the processes of disease and death that anyone who lacks such power seems superfluous or even intrusive in a hospital. And of course in moments of acute medical crisis, when the needed intervention is resuscitation or emergency surgery, the patient needs other services than those the minister can offer. But even when the "crisis" is the more universal and more protracted one of facing mortality or reckoning with the limits of what medicine can and should do, pastors still find it much easier to "stop by" and leave some tangible expression of the church's good wishes than to remain long enough to be themselves the conveyance of the community's concern. Thus they withhold our most powerful and vital testimony to God's presence among us: the face, the voice, the touch of one whom Christ has made our brother or sister.

This does not happen because ministers are unwilling to give patients or parishioners the time it takes to be with them in crisis. The same pastor who is in and out of the hospital in five minutes may be found on the same day spending hours counseling those in trouble or visiting with shut-ins. Still less is it because pastors and chaplains do not care about the pain of the suffering, or the anguish of families making decisions about treatment. It is rather because they do care, but equate caring effectively with curing, something they recognize is beyond their ability. They feel the pain and confusion as something that cries out to be remedied somehow, and yet they feel themselves helpless to do anything to lessen grief or eliminate perplexity. That sense of powerlessness in the face of need is acutely uncomfortable for anyone; for ministers, people trained and expected to be able to help, it can be almost intolerable.

Although it sounds harsh to say so, it must be acknowledged that this intense discomfort is compounded equally of compassion and of the need for personal power. Our sense of having nothing to say, of inadequacy and embarrassment and almost of shame in the face of another's suffering, are a clue that we want and expect to have some kind of answer. Ministers with whom I have spoken of this sometimes remark, "They all look at me as if I'm supposed to help, and I never know what to say." Pastors (and often enough their parishioners) seem to think that pastoral leadership should confer some wisdom to solve the problems of disease and mortality, or at least to lessen the suffering and grief they create. One has only to articulate such a supposition to recognize its absurdity.

What we have to offer one another is not any solution, but chiefly the honesty and humility to acknowledge our shared predicament, and the willingness to endure together pain that we cannot relieve. Sometimes (and only sometimes) we can testify to our own experience of God's care and companionship in the face of fear and sorrow. Sometimes we can affirm the claims and promises of Christian faith with passion and real conviction. Often we can simply read together the laments and celebrations of the psalter, or the doxologies of the epistles which declare and rest in a glory beyond our reckoning. Other times, wounded by grief and shaken by doubts of our own, we can with integrity do no more than "weep with those who weep" (Rom. 12:15). But for the importance of doing even this we have not only the authority of Paul, but the example of Jesus, who has forever shielded such tears from reproach (John 11:32-36).

In some circumstances, there may be additional roles for pastors to play in helping patients and families make concrete decisions about medical care, roles for which this book offers some small preparation. They may be able to provide tools to aid in judgment and a forum in which to think through such decisions. They may even find themselves privileged to be bearers of the kind of insight and clarity which allow us to make even painful decisions with a measure of peace, and bearers of a tradition broad and strong enough to withstand our griefs. But whatever role ministers find themselves called to, whatever tasks they are fitted to fulfill, what they must *not* do is yield to the temptation to cut and run.

The Minister as Interpreter

One of the ways in which a pastor or hospital chaplain may serve a patient/parishioner is by acting as a sort of intermediary between the patient and family on one hand, and the hospital's professional staff on the other. The purpose of this role is simply mutual translation and interpretation. Such a liaison can ensure that the family's questions are understood and answered, and that the patient and family in turn understand what they are told about the medical options facing them. The need for such translation arises in part because of the differences of vocabulary between healthcare givers and lay people, differences that can be bridged by a minister who is willing to pursue explanations and ask questions that families may have difficulty articulating.

But the need for translation arises even more fundamentally because of the very different places that care givers and patients or their families occupy in conversations about treatment. For members of the treatment team, however compassionate and concerned they may be, decisions about particular patients take place in the context of a hundred similar decisions past and future, as part of a larger constellation of professional experiences and judgments. For the patient and his or her family on the other hand, the experience of serious or fatal illness is a unique and emotionally laden crisis point. There is always the present anxiety, strain and grief; these in turn may create a kind of emotional pressure cooker in which old fears and old conflicts rise to shape or to distort the decisions that must be made about care. In such a context few things are obvious, and nothing is routine.

A sensitive interpreter may be able to help patients and their families sort out present issues about treatment from deeper and longer-standing issues about family relationships more generally. She or he may also be able to illuminate for the staff the patient's needs and concerns in ways that greatly improve cooperation between patients, families, and providers, and thus improve the quality of care. On some occasions, when communication and collaboration between staff and patient have broken down, the role of the pastor may be more explicitly that of advocate, working to ensure that the voice of the patient is heard and given attention rather than lost in the welter of institutional policy, hospital procedure, and sheer routine.

In order to serve in these ways, a minister needs certain information and certain skills. To begin with, a pastor or chaplain must have some basic understanding of the clinical language used in patient care: must, for example, know what a gastronomy tube is for, how it works, and what benefits and harms it may bring. This understanding need not be at any highly technical level, but may be gathered by simple common-sense inquiries about the purposes and potential problems of proposed treatments. In principle, all the necessary information should be available in the explanation and description that accompany requests for informed consent; in reality, this material may be lacking, or may itself need explanation.

Thus, a modest amount of self-education may be called for when the minister encounters unfamiliar tools or procedures, or needs to understand more about a patient's condition in order to help explain or evaluate a proposed treatment. But even in these cases, the understanding called for is simply that needed to make sense of the treatment suggested, and to convey its probable results to the patient and family. The contribution of a minister in this role is in clear and sympathetic explanation, not in clinical expertise.

To act as an interpreter and facilitator in discussions of explicitly ethical issues in medicine, a minister must also understand the sort of moral language commonly used in this setting. This is both to comprehend its terms (risk-benefit analysis, autonomy, informed consent and so on), and to be able freely to translate it into a kind of moral conversation more natural to patients and families as they face decisions. One of the purposes of this book is to provide readers with some familiarity with the language of bioethics. (Another is to provide some account of how that language is related to the "native speech" of Christian moral reflection; this second task will be explored further in the following section.)

In this area in particular, the role of intermediary requires a kind of tact. There are complex institutional and role-related boundaries to be honored between patients and staff, between staff members in different locations, and sometimes even between patients and their family members. There are times when all involved in a difficult decision feel a great deal of constraint, and are unable to be candid with each other about their fears, their expectations, or their real convictions. At an even deeper level, there is a terrible privacy imposed on family and patient by the suffering of illness and death, and on family and staff by responsibility for decisions that affect the lives and deaths of other people. There are limits to empathy, and they must be respected; all these are matters for humility, delicacy, and patience.

To be effective in this setting, a pastor has to create a context in which it is safe to tell the truth, and in which the truth that is needed can be borne by those who need to hear it. In particular, a pastor or chaplain must be at ease with the intense emotions and conflicts that arise as people try to come to terms with uncertainty and grief. Obviously, such skills and qualities go far beyond a discussion of pastoral roles in medical crises. Nor are they simply a matter of technique, whether pastoral, ethical, or psychological. Rather, they are part of the ongoing task of personal and spiritual formation which is the permanent vocation of every minister of Jesus Christ.

The roles of interpreter and patient advocate are ones that may, in many cases, be shared with other persons in the health care setting, including social workers, nurses, consulting physicians, or patients' rights advocates appointed by the hospital to serve just this purpose. Occasionally, clinical ethicists who serve on hospital staff or on institutional review boards are asked to consult with patients, family members, or physicians. They may work to clarify the moral issues at stake in a decision, or try to persuade a patient or her family to give consent for a treatment that the staff regards as clearly in a patient's interests. In principle, all of these people may be welcomed as partners in the task of offering patients and their families information, support, and a context for moral conversation about treatment decisions. Often these other professionals bring great skill and compassion to their work, and they have the advantage of clinical information and experience which may be very valuable. However, there are also a number of reasons why a pastor or a hospital chaplain may be an especially apt and accessible person to act as interpreter between healthcare givers and those for whom they care, even though this aspect of the minister's role may be largely secular in its character.

The first advantage of a parish pastor in a hospital setting is that she or he is already known, at least to some degree. Amid a sudden universe of strangers in the form of a rotating staff of interns, residents, and nurses, the minister is a familiar face, and a person with whom some level of trust already exists. (The same may or may not be true of the attending physician, but this role is by its nature more limited in its context, and in the present day is more likely to be fairly formal and relatively impersonal.[2]) The minister also knows the patient in some other context than as a sufferer from illness and an object of care. Thus he or she provides a bridge to the "normal" world and activity that preceded hospitalization, and a reminder of the larger identity of the patient as a person.

Their prior acquaintance gives both pastor and patient some sense of each other's history and circumstances, at least relative to the mutual ignorance of patients and medical staff. For those whose involvement in church is more than marginal, the pastor can also look forward to an ongoing role in the life of the patient and his or her family after the current medical crisis has passed. The knowledge that the relationship in which support is offered has a past and a future which extends beyond the medical context may offer a greater basis for trust. At the same time, it calls on both patient and minister for a commitment to a deeper moral community than is possible in relationships bounded by the hospital setting.

Even a hospital chaplain who is previously unknown to the patient shares some advantages with a parish pastor, as well as bringing some distinct benefits that belong to her or his position. The chaplain shares with pastor and patient the outsider status of being a lay person in the medical community, and the foundation of shared presuppositions rooted in basic Christian commitments. She or he also shares the role of minister, in relation to whom there is social support and permission for acknowledging vulnerability and expressing need. Particular to the role of hospital chaplain is a natural mediating position: the chaplain is a member of the hospital staff, yet one whose training and responsibilities are pastoral and theological rather than medical and scientific. He or she has the advantage of being known to the staff, and of knowing more about their experience and viewpoint than the average parish minister. At the same time, with patients for whom faith is an important part of identity, the chaplain has a kind of "given" connection and credibility. Thus, a chaplain who maintains both professional and personal connections with hospital colleagues, and a vital sense of his or her identity as a servant of the gospel, occupies a unique location for serving as an interpreter and facilitator in conversations between staff and patients.

The Minister as Partner in Discernment

In the previous section, we spoke of roles which might appropriately be taken up by a minister, but which are not particularly "theological" in character, nor limited to those who work from a theological starting point. Now we move into a kind of pastoral function in which the explicit convictions of Christian faith form part of the content of ministry, so to speak. This is the role of the pastor when difficult ethical decisions about treatment must be made by patients or their families: she or he can serve as a partner in the process of moral discernment.

This is a task which involves a kind of critical appropriation of the discipline of medical ethics. One of the ways in which a minister can serve people in medical crisis is to make the tools of bioethics, its principles and methods, available to patients and families as they face complex decisions. (Some of this may already be required in "translating" the language of the hospital staff for patients or parishioners.) Another aspect of that service is to make explicit the connections—and the distinctions—between the ethical understandings of contemporary medicine and the moral consequences of Christian faith. This takes one beyond the task of explaining and interpreting the moral language of the medical profession into a constructive theological task: that of selecting and evaluating and critiquing the profession's way of thinking and speaking in light of the commitments that Christians share.

In Chapter 2, I laid out the distinctive reasons that Christians have for embracing the obligations expressed in the principles of bioethics as their own. There I spoke as well of the limitations or reinterpretations of those principles which are entailed by the affirmations Christians share. In some sense, the role of "partner in moral discernment" is the pastoral dimension or application of the theoretical work that occupied us in Chapter 2. In the pastoral context, of course, such a conversation need not be either comprehensive or systematic, nor will it use the formal language of a book like the present one. Certainly there is no particular need to introduce awkward and alien terms like "non-maleficence." Instead, the minister can address the special vulnerability that comes with illness, and the enormous obligation for the physical and spiritual welfare of those over whom we exercise power.

The pastor can talk with a patient confronting different options in treatment about the genuine freedom of the Christian person, who stands before God graced and empowered by the Holy Spirit, an accountable steward of the gift of life. He or she can speak as well of the character of that freedom as liberty rather than license, and echo Paul's challenge that we not use our liberty as an occasion for sin. In short, such conversation will focus on the particular conflicts or questions that confront a patient or a family in the effort to make, and make peace with, decisions about treatment. The challenge is to talk through issues in a way that reveals the relevance and the force of the things Christians already implicitly believe. This includes things about the worth and the meaning and the limits of human bodily existence, and about the nature of our responsibility for it. It also includes things about the character of Christian moral life as rooted in the life of the community, grounded in worship, and permeated by prayer.

The need to do this kind of work will not always arise. Some decisions about treatment may be painful or difficult to make without being a source of specifically *moral* doubt or confusion. In these situations, it will be enough for the minister to remain present with those facing such decisions, helping them to clarify their reasons for acting and to recognize what course best fulfills their responsibilities. But in cases where there is deep moral uncertainty or conflict, or those in which patients and their families experience a great deal of guilt and anguish about choices which cannot be avoided, such explicit conversation joining medicine and theology may be vital. It can provide a bridge between issues as they are confronted in the medical context, and the commitments and affirmations, the practices and the memories, that sustain the moral lives of Christian people. By entering into such conversation, a minister can help Christians bring the resources of their faith and its community to bear on decisions which threaten to overwhelm them with their weight and difficulty.

As we have already seen,[3] some of the moral dilemmas that arise in the practice of medicine do so because the concrete shape of non-maleficence or justice or some other obligation is difficult to determine amid the uncertainties of actual practice. The success of treatment is unpredictable, the course of a disease is unforeseeable, and so forth. Others arise because obligations flowing from bioethical principles seem to conflict in what they require or prohibit. Honoring patients' choices keeps us from serving their best medical interests, the obligation not to harm particular patients seems to leave others open to injury, and so on. Recasting the conversation against the background narrative of Christian faith can illuminate (without necessarily resolving) both kinds of difficulty.

In the first kind of dilemma, what we confront is simply a particularly poignant and intractable instance of human limitation. It is the reality that we are constrained by ignorance and bound by time. All of our decisions about medical treatment are based upon very well-educated guesses about how a body will react to a given intervention. They rest upon varying degrees of likelihood about the outcome that rarely (if ever) approach certainty. And yet we must act, or our decisions will be made by default in our failure to act. There is no "solution" to the fact of human finitude.

The role of the pastor here may be to hold us to the task, helping us face the necessity of thinking through choices as well as we can amid the unknowns of actual situations. We can count on no special revelation that allows us to sidestep the work of careful consideration about what is possible, what is likely, and what decision we can make faithfully and responsibly. But the story we tell also offers us what may be the only kind of comfort that we can receive in the midst of our uncertainty. In requiring us to understand ourselves as finite and contingent, it gives us permission to acknowledge our limits, and reminds us that ours is the responsibility of creatures and not that of gods. It exhorts us to pursue with due diligence the skill and knowledge and insight we need, in medicine as elsewhere. We are to work for them and to pray for them and to have the humility to seek them from one another. But the same story also presupposes that our limits will remain for all that, and it assures us that our ultimate fate and that of those for whom we care rests with God and not with us. Far from being paralyzed by a sense of our own failings, it is a realistic sense of our limits that allows us to make decisions in situations of uncertainty without self-deception. To use the language of faith, it is because God reigns that we can dare to act, knowing as we do that not every decision can be made with confidence, and that even decisions of which we feel sure may be wrong.

The second kind of dilemma may be even more painful, for what we confront here is not so much our inability to be sure about the future as our inability fully to understand the present. Here we experience a decision as bringing us to a kind of moral impasse, where we do not know how to recognize what we ought to do. The danger is that we may lose confidence not only in our own ability to know our obligations, but in the intelligibility of such obligations altogether. It may come to seem to us that all choices are arbitrary, rooted in nothing more substantial than private intuition or the mere power to choose itself.

The contribution of Christian faith to such dilemmas lies in its capacity to make sense of tragedy and of the irreconcilable nature of goods in a fallen world, without falling back on mere will as the foundation of moral life. Christians recognize that the fabric of the world is rent by the fall, and that the evidence of that tearing is everywhere. Yet they believe the world holds together and will do so until God restores the universe seamless and entire. What Christians rely upon is not the clarity or purity of their own moral judgment, or the incorruptibility of reason, but only the final coherence of the world in God.

We have still the responsibility of thinking through conflicts as well as we can. We need to reflect on what freedoms and what limits there are in the legitimate autonomy of people redeemed by Christ for God's service. We need to consider what understanding of justice can accommodate God's extravagant grace. We need to think about the character and weight of risks and benefits when we understand our sole essential and unassailable good to be our relationship with God who will not leave us. In short, we must engage in the practice of moral reasoning about the duties of medicine within the particular understandings of our situation formed by the story we embrace, and that embraces us. This is the kind of constructive moral conversation in which a pastor can serve as a partner and a guide.

But we also have a means to understand that there may be no answer this side of the world's restoration that avoids either anguish or moral danger. In this in-between time, poised between redemption and consummation, we may well be unable to find our way, forced to fall back upon what light God sheds on our confusion, and finally on the trustworthiness of grace. The minister must testify to the necessity of careful moral reflection, and to its limits—and testify as well to the love and mercy of God who "remembers that we are only dust" (Ps. 103:14).

As an instance of the sort of moral conversation I am recommending, I offer the following excerpt from correspondence between myself and a friend. He had read an earlier, shorter version of my discussion of the case of Mrs. E. (pp. 85–90 above) and took the trouble to write me to express his dissatisfaction with my treatment of it. In doing so, he brought up aspects of his own experience and reflection, and thus I tried to deal with both the theoretical and the personal in my response. I include this exchange because it serves to illustrate both the possibilities and the dangers of the kind of conversation I am proposing, which must combine candor and delicacy.

Dear Sondra,

I recently lost a 98½-year-old grandfather. In talking with my mother (it was her father) during the last weeks of his life, the conversation often turned on "quality of life" issues. There were comments like, "Well, it was clear at Christmas that there was really nothing left in his world that could give him any joy or happiness, and living without joy or happiness isn't really living." We were never faced with the necessity of a decision about radically invasive procedures or "pulling the plug" or withholding artificial nutrition or hydration, but if we had been, the decision would have been made— surely with difficulty and doubt and regret—largely in terms of what "quality of life" would have been possible for him at that point and/or afterwards. To me, there is a pretty clear distinction between the continued existence of a human body and the "quality of life" (whatever substantive content that admittedly ambiguous phrase may carry) of a person.

I would describe Mrs. E.'s decision as having been made in something like those terms. It seems she was convinced that her "quality of life" could never again be what it had once been, and consequently, that her continued physical existence was not an attractive proposition. My father, who is 84, has in recent years frequently talked about his real fear of serious incapacitation and/or a slow, lingering death, which would be both painful and costly (in multiple senses) for him and for all the family. He would far rather die quickly (say, from a heart attack, which is much more likely in his case, since he has a history of heart trouble). Given Mrs. E.'s choices, he might well make Mrs. E.'s decision—and I would understand and support that decision, as did Mrs. E.'s children.

Does that mean that my Christian commitments are somehow less clear, vigorous, or "real" than yours?

✦　　✦　　✦

Dear R.,

You are certainly right that Mrs. E. makes her decision in terms of "quality of life," in fact explicitly so according to her son, from whose account that case is constructed. The particular reasons she gives for her negative assessment are (as I indicated) her inability to engage in her favorite pastimes and especially her feeling of humiliation at being dependent. You write in your letter that Mrs. E. "was convinced that her 'quality of life' could never again be what it had once been, and consequently that her continued physical existence was not an attractive proposition." This is perfectly accurate, both in terms of its understanding of Mrs. E.'s situation and in its representation of her reasoning about it. The question that arises is what she ought to do about it.

From her own perspective, the answer is straightforward. Since her life is not "attractive" or satisfying to her, she sets out to bring it to an end, ideally by a fatal dose of drugs. Since the law and the unwillingness of her physician make that option difficult, she opts instead to refuse first antibiotics and then food and water as the quickest way of ending her life. Both Mrs. E. and the son who writes about her death (at her request) treat what she does as an act of rational suicide.

One would have to be made of stone not to have sympathy for Mrs. E., as for anyone facing disability and inevitable decline. One would have to be irrational not to understand why such a decision makes sense both to Mrs. E. and to her family. But it is not a particularly new or dramatic point to note that Christians have traditionally been opposed to acts which directly aim at death as a means of exiting an unattractive or undesirable life. This opposition is based on a number of commonplace Christian notions about our status as creatures and servants of God, as well as the assumption that suffering is not the worst of all evils, and may not always rightly be avoided. Succinctly, the prohibition of suicide expresses the constraints on what autonomy may authorize if we believe that our lives belong to God and not to us. My point is not that Mrs. E. made the wrong decision for her, that is, from her own point of view. (Although I think it is sad that she finds it impossible to receive needed care, apparently graciously given, without humiliation and despair. An understanding of human dignity which rests upon independent agency *is* too thin, I think.) My point is simply that her decision, and her way of coming to it, leave out of the account a number of things that Christians are committed to by the story they tell and the convictions they affirm.

The idea that we are claimed by and accountable to God and each other, or that we might have a responsibility to care for ourselves in some ways (although not in every possible way) even when we cease to find our lives desirable, does not come up. Neither does the need to seek discernment from other people, both those directly affected by our decisions and those outside. There is no reason why these points should occur to Mrs. E. But there *is* a reason why they should occur to us, and a reason why we should look for questions and habits and dispositions that reflect such concerns in our own deliberations. We believe that we belong wholly to God, that we exist in order to love and serve God and each other, and we have to make our decisions about living and dying accordingly. Such commitments have real teeth, and can entail real hardship and suffering. Their consequences are often difficult and unclear in actual experience. But it seems to me vital that we not talk or think in ways which presuppose that we may simply choose death when life is painful and difficult.

Finally, to address you and your experience directly: Of course you and your family talk about what can still give your ailing grandfather joy. Of course you recognize that when continued life offers none of the human possibilities for which we accord it special protection, we may rightly loose our hold upon it. We may then elect less aggressive medical treatment, or even no treatment at all, and let the death of the body ensue naturally; we may give up our efforts to stave off death. But that is really not the same thing as asking for a lethal dose of morphine. And it is also not the same thing as an individual deciding, "If I cannot do X (which might be anything from walking to piloting a jet), then I will act to bring about my own death, because I am unwilling to accept this limitation." Naturally your father (and my father, also elderly with heart disease and diabetes and a family history of Alzheimer's) would rather die quickly and without a prolonged period of physical and financial dependence. So would we all, I expect. But we need not take that to mean that we are entitled to engineer such a death for ourselves or those we love, or categorically refuse to accept life on any terms other than those we would choose. At least, such a presumption seems to me at odds with the idea that we are to live and die to the glory of God, who remains the Lord and Giver of Life.

I do recognize how complex and painful these decisions are in actual experience. I was personally involved in two of the other cases we discussed, and they were brutal. I do not know how much theological disagreement there may be between us, but whatever our differences, there is no ground for self-righteousness or condemnation on my part, which is clearly how my discussion of Mrs. E.'s case came across to you. I regret that, and will try to do better in the future.

The Minister as Witness to the Gospel

Finally we come to the last of the pastoral roles we will discuss, and to the one that is most deeply dependent on the minister as a person of particular convictions, one who carries the story of a particular community. This is the minister's role as a witness to the Gospel. In one sense this is not strictly a theological task, because it is not especially an intellectual task. To testify to a shared faith is not evangelism or apologetics. It does not call upon the minister to articulate systematically what it means to be a Christian, or to explain what it is that Christians believe. It is rather to speak the language of faith to another for whom it is already familiar, like speaking a beloved native tongue to a fellow exile. It is done not to instruct, but to nourish, to reassure, to delight both speaker and listener with an evocation of the home toward which they both look with longing.

This is no more than a particular aspect or occasion of the pastor's fundamental work, which is indeed the fundamental work of the whole church: to bear witness to what God in Jesus Christ has done, and to nurture and celebrate the life that is made possible by God's gracious act. However, this vocation has a special difficulty and a special urgency in the hospital context, because this is a world in which the language and the habits of thought which form the Christian community, its questions and dispositions, are not only absent, but seem irrelevant.

The hospital is a setting where all energy is directed to finely calculated technical interventions, where people are occupied with devising practical strategies for managing the body's dysfunction. Too often, it is a place where persons are reduced to bodies, and bodies to failing organ systems. Language about God the Creator whose life is breathed into us seems, here, quaint and strange. In the middle of talk about cures and procedures, even the language of healing has an odd ring. Here where death is the enemy, and functions so decisively as the outer limit of human concern, we find ourselves unable to remember quite what we meant about a love from which even death could not separate us. It is not so much that the Christian claims seem false, as that they seem peculiar. The affirmation of Christian faith becomes hard to make, its claims difficult to entertain, because the world it depicts as real becomes difficult to imagine, much less believe in. To stake everything upon the truthfulness of what we profess seems like a terrifying gamble. It is so much easier to accept the unspoken assumptions of the institution, to make our choices like good rational consumers of the commodity health care. Yet it is precisely here in this setting, facing the reality of our vulnerability and the inevitability of our death, that we are called upon to stake everything on the truth of what we read and say and sing in worship: on the love and power of the God in whom we believe.

This may make it clear why a witness to Christian faith in the hospital is vital. It may also persuade many that they, at least, do not have such faith: that they lack the confidence and clarity and especially the certainty to act as such a witness. I remember a young minister at a conference, listening to a discussion of the pastor's role as the bearer of the tradition of faith into situations of medical crisis. At the end, he shook his head and offered the opinion that surely a person facing eternity was entitled to better testimony to the gospel than he could provide! But of course what we offer one another is not simply or even preeminently our own testimony, nor is it our own personal faith and confidence to which we bear witness. Instead, we serve by passing on a body of experience vastly broader and stronger than our own. We retell the story of God's faithfulness to God's people across generations, adding our voices to the chorus because we are inheritors of and participants in a saga that began before our ancestors were born. Like the tiny Jewish children who have never been outside of Brooklyn, we intone, "My father was a wandering Aramean. . ." (Deut. 26:5). And we declare with Simeon that "my eyes have seen your salvation" (Luke 2:30-31), on the strength of evidence presented in a temple that was destroyed while the apostles still preached. Like Paul, we hand on to others what we in our turn have received (cf. 1 Cor. 15:3). There is a certain "objectivity" to the witness which does not vary with our changing subjective confidence, our wavering ability to trust and believe in God.

This does not mean that the minister's own faith, her or his own experience of God's goodness and mercy, is irrelevant. How else but from our own lives with this God do we know what story to turn to, what witnesses to call? How else come as a servant of the gospel except in the character of one who lives in daily dependence upon it? But it *does* mean that the minister is not rendered useless or unqualified by doubt, by confusion or uncertainty or anger about how God who loves us can leave us in so much pain and perplexity. A pastor is not disqualified by the capacity to be struck into silence by the sheer weight of suffering and grief, or by knowing when there is nothing to do but cry out a wordless complaint.

Far from being outside the tradition at such times, we are standing in a long line of believers who have pleaded and accused, argued and doubted and challenged—and brought all their objections to the God whom they could not trust, did not believe, and would not follow. Their wrestling fills the pages of the Old Testament, making up the Psalms of Lament and substantial portions of the writings of the Prophets. One of the most vital testimonies a pastor can offer is evidence of the strength and patience of God who can absorb all our questions. A minister can offer an example of the astonishing freedom of prayer, where nothing is off limits, and no degree of honesty, no anger or despair or fear or rebellion, can shock God. When resignation is a virtue, and not just a cover for despair, it is one won through struggle. The pastor's example can give people permission to do their struggling with God as well as against God, perhaps the only difference between faith and disbelief. Disciples are simply those who can pray, "I believe; help my unbelief" (Mark 9:24).

Finally, the minister comes to bear witness in the flattest possible sense of simply speaking the truth. Sometimes this is done to express real confidence, to tell others the story of what God has done in us for their encouragement; we rightly rejoice in Luther's declaration, "You cannot harm me, for I am baptized!" At other times it is done to forge the confidence that is lacking. We make promises partly to strengthen our resolve to do what we intended, and take solemn vows in public in order that the making of them can nerve us to fulfill them. In the same way, we recite the creeds together both to affirm what we believe, and in order that we may come to believe what we say. We may read together the texts that affirm God's care in suffering, and God's power over death, partly so that the affirmation can help to create in us the confidence it articulates. It is one of the many ways in which we rest upon one another, depending on the faith of those who have gone before us when our own faith is shaken or gone.

And it works. We do in fact find in our common declaration the strength to believe—or at least the courage to behave as if we do while we wait for faith to be renewed. But in times of sorrow or fear, in times of anguish and the felt absence of God, we need the prompting of the community, and its support. Part of the vocation of ministers of the gospel is to serve as representatives of that larger community, people who can stand with us in suffering and still affirm: "I believe in God. . . ."

Conclusion

"Awaiting the Redemption of Our Bodies": The Limits of Medicine and Bioethics

Throughout this book I have been arguing as clearly and persuasively as I can that bioethics is a task for the church. I have talked at some length about the rootedness of Christian ethics in the story of God's grace that Christians tell, and about its location in the community called into being by that grace. I have tried to show some relationship between the formal principles of bioethics and the story that forms the Christian community, and have argued for the importance to that community of the kind of reflection and analysis that bioethics involves. Finally, I have spoken of the help ministers might give to patients and their families when they face medical crises and the moral dilemmas that sometimes accompany them.

In all of this, I have tried to be clear about what *could* and what *could not* be expected from the kind of reflection and analysis we are attempting. The place of moral reflection in general in Christian life is vital, but it is not the first or the central thing. Moreover, the results of ethical analysis are not always clear, and in any case the great majority of our moral problems are not problems with knowing the good, but with doing it. For these reasons, we do well to undertake all projects in Christian ethics with modest ambitions. But in the realm of bioethics, these general caveats are not enough. In this context where the stakes are so high and the questions so perplexing, where our emotions are so deeply engaged and our desire for clarity and certainty is so intense, it is necessary to say more about the things we cannot do in order to avoid distorting those things we can.

The particular need to be clear about the limits of what can be done in medical ethics arises from the character of the two enterprises that intersect here. On one side, we have the practice of medicine, itself a marriage of science and art, of career and vocation, with its own internal standards as well as a powerful moral and practical impact on our society. The last fifty years of research and practice have seen an unprecedented increase in our knowledge of the precise working of organs and bodily systems. With it has come a proportionate increase in our ability to intervene in the processes of disease and death. Thus, contemporary physicians have a power to rescue, to cure or to prolong life in the presence of disease, that their historical predecessors could hardly have imagined.

On the other side we have ethics, a field that has grown dramatically in its currency in public conversation and especially in its independence from other activities. Once upon a time "ethics" consisted largely of knowing how to behave in our various roles. It was wedded firmly to *ethos*, that is to particular contexts and to groups of people engaged in particular tasks. There were ways of behaving appropriate to parents, and others appropriate to children, and others expected of teachers or soldiers or even friends. In the absence of much self-conscious scrutiny, these ways of behaving seemed to be more-or-less taken for granted. This is not to say that people did not violate them all the time. There is certainly no reason to suppose that child abuse or the misuse of academic authority or military misconduct are any more common now than they were a hundred years ago. What was different was the degree of apparent consensus that backed standards of behavior, whether these were honored in the breach or the observance.

This is not an indulgence in nostalgia, a hearkening back to the time when "everybody knew what was right." In fact, the moral consensus of the past was achieved partly by excluding from the conversation anyone whose different experience might lead them to different conclusions, and it tolerated a great deal of nonsense and abuse. This is simply an observation about the new prevalence of self-conscious deliberation and debate about standards of behavior. In a society lacking shared presuppositions and widely accepted role definitions, ethics becomes the enterprise in which we try to achieve unity and coherence in moral conduct by means of reason and social agreements. Unfortunately, when morality is wholly detached from tasks—even such generalized and universal tasks as living a good life or being a good citizen—it is hard to justify rules and expectations for behavior. Norms seem arbitrary because there is no accepted purpose toward which they point, and no shared ground on which to build. This is the difficulty with a "neutral" ethic, one detached from any religious or philosophical understanding of existence which might serve as a ground for making judgments about character or conduct.

In this context, two forces come together to create a great demand for medical ethics, and high expectations for what it can accomplish. One is the need to direct and control the enormous and growing power of biomedical technique. The other is the need for some kind of moral basis for social cooperation and collaboration. These are compelling motivations. But to enter upon the task of thinking about the moral obligations of medicine as a Christian is to do so with considerably chastened expectations, both for medicine and for ethics. It is to recognize that bioethics is an undertaking which operates under a sort of double futility, a pair of limits which no technical or theoretical advance can remove. They are sin and mortality.

The fact is that medicine, understood as an activity of saving and prolonging life, is inevitably and absolutely a losing battle. No one survives; no one emerges unscathed; every patient is lost eventually. It is true that we have reduced infant mortality to low levels (although our inner cities are a scandalous exception). We have greatly reduced the number of those who die in childhood or early adulthood of contagious diseases or systemic infections. We have devised effective surgical and medical treatments for everything from some forms of cancer to diabetes and heart disease. As a result, life expectancy in the affluent and industrialized countries of the West and parts of Asia has climbed into the 70s and 80s. But the truth is that we are not much more satisfied with "three score years and ten" than we were with 20 or 40 or 50 years.

It is true that sometimes the physical and mental decline of the sick or the elderly is such that they (and we) come to see death as not only inevitable but welcome. But it is welcomed not as death precisely, but rather as the only possible end to suffering. What we want for those we love is not that they die and be lost to us, or just that they cease to suffer. We want them to be restored to vitality and presence and to the unique constellation of gifts and quirks and even weaknesses that made them who they were to us. Even when we do not doubt that the dead rest safe in God, that in God their ultimate fulfillment is secured, we feel their dissolution and loss not only as a grief but almost as an affront.

And it is not clear that we ought to feel any differently than we do. Most of us can thoroughly sympathize with, even if we feel constrained not to echo, the protest of Edna St. Vincent Millay's "Dirge Without Music":

> Down, down, down into the darkness of the grave
> Gently they go, the beautiful, the tender, the kind;
> Quietly they go, the intelligent, the witty, the brave.
> I know. But I do not approve. And I am not resigned.[1]

At best, we are deeply conflicted. On the one hand, to accept our status as embodied and contingent creatures is to accept the bodily limit of death. Moreover, believing that God is our final good, the "one thing needful" in whom all our needs and blessings converge, we are to do even our mourning in patience and in hope. On the other hand, our tradition gives more than a suggestion that death, at least in its power to isolate and alienate us from one another, *is* a kind of affront: a sign that something in God's good creation has gone awry. How else are we to make sense of the claim that death entered the world by sin, as life is restored by the righteousness of Christ (Rom. 5:12-20)? How else to understand the declaration that the last enemy to be conquered by Christ is death itself (1 Cor. 15:26), so that in the eschatological presence of God, death will be no more (Rev. 21:3-4)? Death is rightfully seen as an enemy of sorts; more than a mechanical failure of organic systems, it is a sign of the reign of sin over the world. But it is a reign we are powerless to break, and until it finally is broken, all the efforts of medicine are like the rearguard action of a retreating army; to be done effectively, it must be done under the presumption of impending (if not final) defeat.

And thus we come to the other limiting reality which constrains what we may hope for in our practice of bioethics. This is the fact that in all our care, in all our treatment of the sick, in all our wrestling with what we may or must or ought to do in medicine, we act as sinners and under the conditions of sin, both personal and systemic. This means that we operate as people whose perception of reality is clouded by illusions: as those whose judgments about all the people and things we encounter in the world are distorted by self-interest and obscured by self-deception. There is no trick of methodology that will overcome our moral limits as decision-makers. It also means that we act within the constraints of a world where sin—not only violence and hatred but our everyday indifference to one another, with all of its structural and economic manifestations—is commonplace. It is a world in which personal and social evils converge to create situations in which none of the courses of action open to us can be embraced as good: a world where "goods collide and evils gather."

Examples in the realm of bioethics are distressingly common. How do we care for and heal and protect a pregnant rape victim? To terminate the pregnancy seems like an example of "visiting the sins of the fathers upon the children," yet who can say that the victim "ought" to endure the burdens of carrying and bearing the child as well as the violence done to her? On another front, how do we weigh the claim that every child has to be protected and cherished and helped to achieve her full potential against the brute fact that no one wants a particular handicapped newborn? How aggressively do we intervene to save the life of such an infant when we know that all the state facilities available to care for the child are essentially warehouses for human discards? To register such conflicts is not to suggest that we throw up our hands in despair and declare that, since all choices are bad, it matters not which we choose. Such a course would be cowardly and self-indulgent. But it is vital that we recognize what will and what will not yield to analysis, what can and what cannot be looked for from our application of this (or any) method of moral reflection to the task of caring for the sick.

The point of stressing the limits posed by sin and death for the project of medical ethics is not to undermine and cast doubt on the utility of either medicine or ethics; it is rather to protect them from distortion. For unless we reckon truthfully with the conditions under which we operate, we risk perverting the practices both of medicine and morality. Part of discerning what we ought to do is keeping always before us what is possible for us to do, and what is a delusion. When the goal of medicine is taken—overtly or tacitly—to be staving off death for as long as possible, what results is a distorted medicine. A balanced view of mortality, which sees death as a real enemy temporarily victorious, guards against both the premature embrace of death and its desperate (and hopeless) avoidance. Such a view helps us remember that the central function of medicine is not to preserve life indefinitely, but rather to care for it responsibly, exercising real but limited power. Death is to be resisted, but only within the limits imposed by the truth about ourselves and each other—a truth which includes mortality, and God's gracious sovereignty over all life.

Similarly, we must recognize that ethics, as a disciplined process of moral reflection, cannot serve to eliminate difficulty or obscurity, much less to guarantee goodness. It serves only to help us to see and to think—and ultimately to love—as well as we can. Understanding ethics as a discipline and a tool does protect us from an irresponsible emotivism—the popular modern position that ends all moral debates with "well, this is what I feel good about." But it protects us as well from a sort of naive formalism that supposes that the results of moral analysis constitute the good rather than merely helping (sometimes) to reveal it. Such a view neglects the truth that no method is more reliable than the one who employs it, and all we have to employ this set of methods and tools are the sinners we declare ourselves to be.

For all this, careful and ongoing ethical analysis of what constitutes faithful care for the sick is neither insignificant nor optional. Part of what it means to be in God's image as knowing and loving creatures who choose is to be responsible. As stewards of life, we must account for what we do, and for what we leave undone, in the protection and the nurture and the ultimate relinquishment of the gift of our bodily existence. To do so without making use of all the tools at our disposal—without the best medical information we can obtain, without the most rigorous standards of intellectual clarity, without the deepest examination of our fears and desires and motives—would be to act irresponsibly. Medical ethics, with all of its ambiguities, is an activity for the in-between in which the church now lives: the time between redemption and reunion, the time between the promise and its full manifestation, the time between hope and sight. Entering into its tasks as Christians, and offering its insights to one another as pastors and fellow disciples, is part of how we care for one another "while we wait for adoption, the redemption of our bodies" (Rom. 8:23), and for the realization of John's vision:

> Behold, the dwelling of God is among mortals. He will dwell with them as their God, and they will be his people. And God himself will be with them, and he will wipe every tear from their eyes. Death will be no more; mourning and crying and pain will be no more, for the former things have passed away. (Rev. 21:3-4, AT)

Notes

Notes to Introduction

1. Throughout this book, I will use the terms *medical ethics* and *bioethics* more or less interchangeably. This is not strictly accurate, since bioethics is a broader term than medical ethics, embracing questions such as the moral status of animals in research or the ethics of intervention in non-human living systems. I might instead use the term biomedical ethics for greater precision, but it is cumbersome and unfamiliar to most people.

Notes to Chapter 1

1. Although these are my own starting assumptions about Christian ethics, there is nothing particularly original in this account of the role of the story. This formulation is indebted to Stanley Hauerwas, *A Community of Character* (Notre Dame: University of Notre Dame Press, 1981).

2. I will focus on the New Testament because these are the constitutive texts of the Christian community, and because our space is limited. In fact, Christian tradition has always read the two Testaments together, insisting that each is to be understood in light of the other. The Old Testament is presupposed here as well.

3. In fact, from this standpoint the concept of a "right to life" can be endorsed only with considerable reservation. It must be understood as a claim against attack which is founded not on our ownership of ourselves, but on the premise that life is holy in the flat-footed sense of belonging to God and not to us.

4. I am acutely aware as I write this that the "we" whose lives are relatively less dangerous and difficult include not all Christians, but only the majority of those living in the affluent and industrialized nations of North America, Europe, and parts of Asia. However, these are the places where medical technology is available, and thus where decisions about its use must be made. It is in this cultural and material context that this conversation about bioethics takes place.

5. (Matt. 16:21; Matt. 17:12; Mark 8:31; Mark 9:12; Luke 9:22; Luke 24:26; etc.)

Notes to Chapter 2

1. Sherwin B. Nuland, *How We Die: Reflections on Life's Final Chapter* (New York: A. A. Knopf, 1994).

2. Although these words (or their Greek equivalents) do not appear in the ancient form of the Hippocratic oath, there is a promise to keep the sick from harm, and to refrain from "intentional injustice and mischief."

3. This is an obligation honored as often in the breach as in the observance, unfortunately. However, the persistence of our feeling that there is something wrong with people being denied care because they lack funds is evidence of the enduring power of this covenantal model of health care, despite the enormous commercialization of medicine in recent decades.

4. Jehovah's Witnesses understand the reception of blood transfusions as a kind of "consuming" or eating blood, forbidden in the holiness code of Leviticus (17:10). This seems to be based on very early medical texts which referred to transfusions as a form of "alimentation," because blood is what carries nutrients to body tissue.

5. See p. 42.

6. This is one form of the problems surrounding judgments of competence; see pp. 42–44.

7. In their 1993 legislative affairs document distributed to their membership. It should be noted that the AMA Ethics committee has stated that these principles should not be taken to permit "invidious discrimination" against certain patient populations.

8. This is well documented. See, for example James Allen, "Health Care Workers and the Risk of HIV Transmission," in *Hastings Center Report* (April/May 1988): 2–5.

9. There are, of course, voluntary actions which have predictable effects on health. We know, for instance, that smoking, alcohol consumption, and the use of illegal drugs can cause damage or death. This has led to some proposals to exclude "self-induced" illnesses from publicly funded care. The difficulty is in sorting out the weight of various contributing factors in illness, and in the degree of intrusiveness it would require to exclude the effects of all bad choices from care. Would we review the diets of people with heart disease or high blood pressure, and refuse to treat those with poor habits? Would we penalize those who took risky jobs, or engaged in sports with a high injury rate? When it comes to applying such tests consistently, most people decide it is impracticable.

Notes to Chapter 3

1. The words used by the physician in Case #1 below.

2. There is always a tendency with elderly patients for hospital staff to defer too early to the family's wishes, even while the patient is conscious

and capable of participating directly in treatment decisions. This is partly due to the uncertainties of determining competence, and to the fear of pressure or litigation from dissatisfied families. But it is also due to the fact that in these situations, the family is often much easier for the physician to identify with and communicate with than is the older and severely ill patient.

3. To regard death as a call does not require that we regard God as the agent of death, or try to conceive how God could desire that this victim of violence die of his wounds, or that toddler be killed in a car accident. The world is fallen, "subjected to futility" in Paul's powerful phrase (Rom. 8:20), and both moral evil and natural accidents are real facts which cause real suffering and devastation. Unless we deny both human moral freedom and all natural causality, we must accept that God does not shield us from harm, and that is not what we count on when we entrust ourselves and those we love to God's care. God enters into our suffering, and promises ultimately to vindicate our trust, but that vindication is eschatological, coming when "the creation will be set free from its bondage to decay" (Rom. 8:21). What Christians affirm is resurrection, not protection from death.

4. Presentation adapted from the article by David Eddy, "A Conversation with My Mother," *Journal of the American Medical Association*, Vol. 272, No. 3 (July 20, 1994): 179–81.

5. The assertion made by David Eddy, the son of the patient, in his discussion of her death, ibid., 180.

6. This pastoral focus has disadvantages as well, of course. In particular, the emphasis on individual cases leaves to one side enormous and pressing questions of public policy, particularly in the area of health care financing and allocation, to which Christian construals of justice and of human community can make distinctive and important contributions.

Notes to Chapter 4

1. From a lecture given by Ms. L'Engle at Yale Divinity School in the spring of 1986.

2. This should not be taken as a criticism, nor is it by any means always the case; I have seen physicians weep for the suffering of patients they could not help, and grieve deeply with those facing death.

3. In the theoretical discussion of Chapter 2 and the cases of Chapter 3.

Note to Conclusion

1. From *Edna St. Vincent Millay: Collected Lyrics* (New York: Harper & Row, 1979), p. 172.

Suggestions for Further Reading

Beltran, Joseph E. *The Living Will and Other Life and Death Medical Choices*. Nashville: Thomas Nelson, 1994.

Written by a Presbyterian minister and chaplain, this book is very concrete and practical, focusing on discussion of cases and issues regarding treatment at the end of life. It includes some brief discussion of the theological and theoretical bases for the positions it takes and the actions it recommends, but is more interested in offering resources and suggestions for pastors and lay people about advanced directives, health care powers of attorney, etc. Very accessible and helpful on practical pastoral concerns, it is less helpful in resolving the many open questions that it identifies.

Bouma, Hessel, et al. *Christian Faith, Health, and Medical Practice*. Grand Rapids: Wm. B. Eerdmans, 1989.

This is the longest and most comprehensive of the works listed here. However, it will reward the interested reader with careful and balanced moral and theological analysis of a wide range of topics. It is the joint product of five authors representing the disciplines of biology, medicine, sociology, philosophy, and theological ethics, and includes extensive references and useful appendices. Good, non-technical writing makes this volume available to clergy and lay readers.

Hauerwas, Stanley. *Suffering Presence*. Notre Dame: University of Notre Dame Press, 1986.

This collection of essays is accurately described by the author as having as much to do with political and social theory as with matters usually thought of as medical ethics. Nevertheless, its reflections on suffering (essay 1) and its discussions of death, suicide, and medical experimentation (Part II) are interesting and provocative, and cast some light on what difference Christian convictions make in these areas. The writing is not always as clear as one might wish, but the examples are vivid and the general argument can be followed by a patient reader without special background.

Hilton, Bruce. *First, Do No Harm: Wrestling with the New Medicine's Life and Death Dilemmas.* Nashville: Abingdon Press, 1991.

A very basic and readable book, with the emphasis on the right of patients and their families to make their own decisions in matters of medical treatment. Aimed at opening up the questions rather than at providing answers, it sometimes sets up problems in ways that oversimplify what is at stake, partly because it introduces more issues than can be dealt with in its 140 pages. Nevertheless, it is a useful beginning point for discussion.

Kelly, David F. *Critical Care Ethics: Treatment Decisions in American Hospitals.* Kansas City: Sheed and Ward, 1991.

This book explores some of the controversies over what kind of treatment may be withdrawn or withheld in terms of the exiting tradition of Roman Catholic medical ethics. It argues for using the already established concepts of "ordinary" or "extraordinary" treatment, based on the balance of benefits and burdens treatment entails. Later sections deal with pain management and with pastoral roles in aiding the dying. Provides useful and easy to understand review of some of the court cases that have shaped law and social policy in matters of treatment termination.

Kilner, John. *Life on the Line: Ethics, Aging, Ending Patients' Lives, and Allocating Vital Resources.* Grand Rapids: Wm. B. Eerdmans, 1992.

Clearer and more careful about its methodological and theological commitments than many works in this area, this book may provoke disagreement but will be illuminating for its critics as well as for those who agree with the views it expresses. An extensive first section makes a general methodological proposal for Christian ethics, and latter sections explore the relevance of this approach for issues in end of life and allocation decisions. The writing is straightforward and accessible.

Wennberg, Robert N. *Terminal Choices: Euthanasia, Suicide, and the Right to Die.* Grand Rapids: Wm. B. Eerdmans, 1989.

A very detailed and precise analysis of the morality of ending life written by a professor of philosophy who is also an ordained Presbyterian minister. He makes use of both theological and philosophical resources in writing that is abstract without being technical. A valuable presentation of a broad Christian view which will repay careful attention.

In addition to these resources, a series of books published under the auspices of **The Park Ridge Center for Health, Faith, and Ethics** looks at issues of medical ethics from the standpoint of different religious traditions. Volumes include:

Holifield, E. Brooks. *Health and Medicine in the Methodist Tradition: Journey Toward Wholeness.* New York: Crossroad, 1986.

Marty, Martin E. *Health and Medicine in the Lutheran Tradition: Being Well.* New York: Crossroad, 1983.

McCormick, Richard A. *Health and Medicine in the Roman Catholic Tradition: Tradition in Transition.* New York: Crossroad, 1984.

Smith, David H. *Health and Medicine in the Anglican Tradition: Conscience, Community, and Compromise.* New York: Crossroad, 1986.

Vaux, Kenneth L. *Health and Medicine in the Reformed Tradition: Promise, Providence, and Care.* New York: Crossroad, 1984.

In these volumes, writers who are expert representatives of these various religious communities present both historical and contemporary perspectives on their own traditions' characteristic methods and contributions. These essays are both descriptive and constructive, noting deficiencies as well as praising accomplishments. Intended for non-specialists, these are excellent resources for pastors or chaplains who want to pursue more detailed knowledge of their own faith community's reflections on matters of health care and ethics.

From 1986 through 1995, the Park Ridge Center published a quarterly journal, *Second Opinion*, which dealt with the intersection of health, faith, and ethics. Issues of the journal were organized topically, and included essays and commentaries as well as extended case studies written by people from a wide variety of perspectives and professional fields. Back issues of *Second Opinion* and other related materials can be obtained from:

The Park Ridge Center
211 E. Ontario St., Suite 800
Chicago, IL 60611
Phone: (312) 266-2222
Fax: (312) 266-6086

The Center for Bioethics and Human Dignity brings Christian perspectives to bear on a wide range of bioethical issues. It publishes an international journal, *Ethics and Medicine*, and offers newsletters, books, audio tapes, video tapes, and other printed and computer-based resources. For more information and a list of resources, contact:

> The Center for Bioethics and Human Dignity
> 3065 Half Day Road
> Bannockburn, IL 60015
> Phone: (847) 317-8180
> Fax: (847) 317-8141